11B10

MEMORIES OF A LIGHT WEAPONS INFANTRYMAN IN VIETNAM

JOHN MAGNARELLI

Riverhaven Books

www.RiverhavenBooks.com

11B10 is a historical memoir; all materials are from the author's recollections and personal photos.

Published in the United States by Riverhaven Books

ISBN: 978-1-951854-28-7

Author photo credit: John Daley

ACKNOWLEDGEMENTS

These stories are recollections of my time in the service, especially my year in Vietnam, along with some other musings. The stories started from an online course in memoir writing through the Duxbury, MA Senior Center with the idea I would leave a legacy to my sons Christopher and Patrick. It then blossomed into a larger project as I recalled more and more details. The stories reflect what almost three million men and eleven thousand women went through during the mid-to-late '60s, as a small police action in an unheard of Southeast Asian country developed into one of the most turbulent times in our nation's history. I hope that anyone who served in Vietnam and reads these stories will recall his or her own time in country and relate to what I have written. And for those who never served in the military I hope you will have a better understanding of what many of us went through.

I'd like to thank Brooke McDonough and the Duxbury Senior Center for facilitating this memoir writing course as well as the rest of my Zoom mates for the encouragement we had for each other's stories. Also, an acknowledgement to the Jamaica Plain, MA Veterans Administration for all the work they do in providing health services to our many veterans and especially to Sarah Krill Williston and her department for their award-winning work in servicing veterans with Post Traumatic Stress Disorder. Of course to my parents, Romeo and Jennie Magnarelli, for a lifetime of love and support. And finally a very special thank you goes to my wife Pam who expertly edited this material.

FRED,
Best wishes and hope
you enjoy the book
Sincerely
John Magnarelli

661/750

Dedicated to the 58,220 men and women
who paid the ultimate sacrifice;
May they always be remembered

TABLE OF CONTENTS

FIRST DAY IN THE SERVICE

I was 19 years old and had traveled out of the state of Massachusetts just once in my young life. I knew this day was coming as most guys my age did. I had friends who had been in the service and coming from a predominately blue-collar town it was basically a rite of passage. A year earlier six of my close friends, Billy Cotter, Jack Lavery, Mark and Al Bartoloni, Dan McCarthy and Jimmy Monahan, had all enlisted in the Army together and left on the same day. I made a value judgment, the first of many as my life went on, to opt to get drafted instead of enlisting. Like with many decisions, I weighed the pros and cons. If I enlisted I could choose my military occupation specialty. I could be a clerk, a cook, a mechanic, a truck driver or any other non-combatant job that I wanted. There was also a good chance that I would not have to go to Vietnam. The downside of enlisting was that it was a three-year commitment. If I waited to get drafted I was assured of becoming an infantryman and doing a year tour of duty in Vietnam. The upside of getting drafted was it was only a two-year commitment. Putting it down on paper makes me wonder why I chose the latter.

So here it is - induction day. I had been working in a factory, Mathewson Machine Works, as a drill press operator since I graduated from high school. It was a solid job and I had fallen into a comfortable routine. However, a month earlier I had received my letter from the draft board ordering me to report for induction on August 12, 1968. Little did I know what a profound change that letter would have on my life. If I hadn't been drafted I probably would have been content to continue working in the factory, never go to college, and not have the career I enjoyed or the family I love.

That morning I left home with my dad driving me to the South Boston Army Base where all new recruits were processed into the service. There was no big send off, he just dropped me off on his way to work like we did every morning. This time he shook my hand and said, "Good luck and stay safe." The South Boston Army Base is an imposing building, a remnant of World War II. There are long halls painted a dull gray with mismatched outdated furniture where thousands of men and women cycled through on their way to military bases across the country. I was there among hundreds of similar guys who were waiting to take their physical and be assigned their basic training orders. I, like everyone else, passed the physical with ease as the Army was rejecting very few. The place was filled with nervous energy. There was a mixture of recruits: three-year enlistees, National Guard and Army Reservists, and then men like me who were drafted. We talked at length among ourselves wondering what awaited us. For the National Guard and reservists, it was a short two-month basic training followed by a two-month specialized training, then back home to serve out their six-year commitment with a once-a-month weekend drill and a two-week summer camp. For the rest of us, we were facing a scary unknown. For most of the morning we encountered what we would all learn was the military way, "hurry up and wait." We would hustle off to one room where we would get a quick instruction and then wait for an hour before we were hustled off to another room. I eventually took the oath that officially enlisted me in the Army and then finally learned that I would be doing my basic training at Fort Jackson, South Carolina. I got on a military bus and headed over to Logan Airport where I would be taking only my second airplane trip ever.

I once thought air travel exotic, but it is quite different when you get onboard a two-engine propeller plane that makes stops in New Jersey, Washington DC, and North Carolina to pick up other recruits before arriving in Columbia, South Carolina. Another bus takes us from the airport to Fort Jackson while we are still wearing civilian clothes. It hasn't quite hit me yet that I am officially in the Army. Once we arrive at Fort Jackson, we exit the bus to a number of pleasant sergeants who warmly greet us and help us along. The first thing we learn is that there is no more walking. Anywhere we went, it was in double-time. Double-time is somewhere between a fast walk and running. Our first stop is the commissary where a fine tailor looks us up and down and decides what size clothes we wear. I do a quick change into olive drab and stuff the remaining fatigues, socks, underwear, field jacket, raincoat, winter coat, and dress greens into a duffle bag. It is August in South Carolina, and I don't quite understand why we are being issued a heavy field jacket and winter coat, but I am not about to ask. The next stop is the hair salon where the waiting barbers take a perverse delight in shaving off the long tresses of the new recruits. After some fine dining in the mess hall, it is nearing 9:00 pm or 2100 hours military time, and we are introduced to our living quarters for the next eight weeks: a one-story barracks with 10 sets of bunk beds on each side of the hall.

Sleep comes easily as I finally realize "I am in the Army now" and wonder what the future has in store for me.

A DAY IN THE LIFE

Many times over the years people have asked me what it was like being in the Army, especially what boot camp was like. We have all seen movies that depict the crusty old drill sergeant who mentally and sometimes physically abuses the raw recruits to toughen them up for battle. Because it is Hollywood, everything is embellished. And because the Army, like most of life, is fairly dull and routine, no one wants to watch a movie about that. I will say that there is some measure of hazing and verbal insults, but it's not quite up to the level you see in the movies. Following is my best recollection of what a typical day was like in boot camp.

Fort Jackson was built in 1917 and is named after Andrew Jackson the 7th President of the United States. It is officially designated as an US Army Infantry Training Center. It functions similar to a large community in that there are over 20,000 people who live and work in its 2,500 buildings. The base is 82 square miles and like a community has churches, athletic fields, swimming pools, golf courses, bowling alleys, banks, a hospital, and a fire station, most of which we will not come in contact with. However, unlike a community it has over 100 infantry training areas that include 50 firing ranges.

My home for eight weeks is a well-worn barracks that is 50 years old. The one-story building is an open concept with 10 sets of bunk beds in a row on each side of a hall that will accommodate the 40 men in my platoon. We awaken at 0530, not to the gentle tones of a radio alarm clock, but to a drill sergeant walking down the middle of the barracks screaming, "It's time to get up, boys and girls!" We quickly use the bathroom, brush our teeth, get dressed and make our bunks. At 0550 the whole platoon hustles out of the barracks and lines up with the three other platoons that make up our company and get the orders of the day. That doesn't take long and then it is double time to a large parade ground where we meet up with other companies to engage in our daily physical training. The Army has designed a training regimen that is called the "daily dozen." It is 12 exercises with 12 repetitions done twice. The exercises consist of jumping jacks, pushups, sit ups, squat thrusts, knee bends, toe touches and a number of others I can't remember. It is then double time back to our company area where we line up for breakfast. Again, double time is something between a brisk walk and a jog and it is the only way we move throughout the day.

Breakfast is at 0700 and contrary to popular belief Army meals are very good. The ingredients are fresh, the menus varied and the end product is nutritious. Everyone gets the same portion size so those who need to lose or gain weight do so. There is also no plate waste as a sergeant dutifully stands by the trash barrel to make sure that everyone finishes his entire meal.

After breakfast it is off to the first training session of the day. Many think that military training only consists of physical activities and weaponry. Obviously that is a major component, but actually the overall training is varied and much like attending school. The training sessions are usually a 60–90-minute block of instruction on any number of topics and then it is off to the next one. As it is "basic training" we only get a general introduction to the topic. As an example, there will be a few sessions on hand-to-hand combat and after those three hours we are confident that we can hold our own with Chuck Norris. A few more sessions on first aid and we are ready for the operating room at Mass General. They actually teach us how to perform a tracheotomy in the field using an ink pen. I don't think so. Bayonet training is where we go at it with a fellow trainee using padded pole devices called pugil sticks to simulate our last-ditch effort to fight off the enemy when we run out of ammunition. It's actually fun as we pair off and beat the hell out of each other without getting hurt. It turns into a competition with everyone cheering each other on and is forever etched in our mind as the drill instructor yells, "How many types of bayonet fighters are there" and the response in unison is "the quick and the dead."

To me one of the most impressive sessions was on camouflage. Here we are, 40 guys sitting on a metal bleacher having a drill instructor lecture us on the basics of deception and blending in. For the first 20 or so minutes it was pretty boring and the platoon was losing interest. All of a sudden what we thought was a bush next to the instructor starts shaking and a soldier who had been lying undetected right in front of us slowly rises up. That gets our attention, and then a pile of leaves on the other side of the instructor starts to move and another hidden soldier stands up, followed by two more located within 20-30 meters of us. Needless to say we were impressed.

What follows is one of those "life lessons" stories. We had just finished a training session and were waiting in formation to head to our next one. I forget what the session was, but we were in the middle of nowhere. The drill sergeant calls us to attention and indicates that he needs a volunteer for some special assignment. He then proceeds to ask us "you are all willing to volunteer, correct?" The response in unison is a resounding "drill sergeant, yes, drill sergeant." He then has to decide who the best man for the job is. He asks anyone who has gone to college to step forward. Of the 40 recruits about 10 go to the front of the formation. He then pares it down by asking who has actually graduated from college. Three stay and the others go back into formation. He then asks each of the remaining three from what college they graduated. Two respond with fairly non-descript schools while the third answers "Princeton University." The drill sergeant has a look of surprise and replies "Well, Mr. Princeton, this is your lucky day. I want you to go over to the latrine and pull out the two s#%t cans, pour gasoline into them, light them on fire, and stir the contents with a broom stick until all the s#%t disappears. The rest of the platoon can take a 15-minute smoke break." So the moral of the story is, before you volunteer for something, make sure you know what you are getting into.

There are additional sessions covering topics like military justice where we learn what NOT to do, drill and ceremony where we learn to march with precision, gas chamber where we enter a tent filled with tear gas and are ordered to take off our mask and sound off with name, rank and serial number before we can exit, and of course a significant number of sessions on firing and qualifying with our M-14 rifle. I, like many of the recruits had never fired a gun before so learning the basics were quite interesting. I also learned quickly that you never referred to a rifle as a gun. If you did a sergeant would order you to run laps around the platoon area holding the rifle upraised in one hand while your other hand grabbed onto your private parts while you yelled out "this is my rifle and this is my gun, one is for killing and one is for fun." Needless to say you quickly got the point. Your M-14 training began on the 25-meter range where you learned the basics of how to zero, sight and aim your weapon as well as the various firing positions. After a number of sessions, you then move to the field firing range where you engage dark silhouetted pop-up targets placed at distances from 70 to 300 meters that are centrally controlled to appear and disappear at various sequences. After mastering the field firing exercises, it is time to qualify for your marksmanship badge. There are three levels of marksmanship: Marksmen, Sharpshooter, and Expert. The qualifying test involves firing 56 rounds at targets anywhere from 50 to 350 meters apart. To be a Marksman you needed to hit 32 of the 56 targets, a Sharpshooter 42 out of 56, and to qualify as an Expert you needed to hit 50 out of 56. I made the Expert level.

After the morning sessions which go from 0800 to 11:30 we then double time back to our company area for lunch, and then are off to the afternoon training that lasts from 1300 to 1700. So far doesn't this sound easy? What you don't realize are the subtle nuances that fill the empty time between training sessions. You build up endurance and conditioning with all the double timing. If not double timing you are marching in precision to enhance teamwork. There is no idle chatter and if a drill sergeant sees you glance the wrong way it is pushups for everyone. All this is to instill discipline and emphasize the attention to detail that could save your life someday. After all this we head back to the company area for dinner that usually is over by 1800.

Now if you think we are done for the day you are mistaken. The next thing we do is take a quick shower. Everyone has to get his shower done by 1830 so that one of the four squads can begin cleaning the bathroom to pass inspection that evening. The other three squads have similar cleaning details like sweeping, mopping, and buffing the floors, polishing the brass fixtures, washing the windows, and policing the grounds around the barracks. When we are not cleaning we are shinning our boots, polishing our belt buckles and arranging the items in our foot and wall lockers to also pass inspection. Our wall locker contains all of our clothes: four sets of fatigue shirts and pants, a field jacket, raincoat, winter coat and dress uniform all arranged in a specific order. The footlocker has our underwear, socks, T-shirts and toiletries, again all folded and arranged in a specific order. At 2030 the drill sergeants enter the barracks for inspection. They look at every nook and cranny of the building and into everyone's lockers. Invariably they find something wrong that results in pushups for an individual, squad or the entire platoon. This is done for effect as everyone knows the building is spotless and all lockers are consistent. It is just another way to instill discipline and have people get into a routine that attends to detail.

It is now 2100 and we finally have our own time. This is when we write a letter home, read a manual or just get to know the rest of the guys in our platoon. As most of us are only 18 or 19 years old and have never been far from home, it is a great learning experience becoming friends with guys from all over the country. Charlie Mosher from Millis, Massachusetts

Charlie Mosher on the right

was someone in my platoon who I became close with and kept in touch with for a number of years after getting out of the service. We were also reunited at Fort Benning for Combat Leadership School. And to show that it is a small world, there was Steve Elios whose father "Phil the Greek" worked with me at Mathewson Machine Works before I was drafted.

At 2200 it is lights out and we do the same thing tomorrow starting at 0530.

Like I said, this is not Hollywood movie material, but it is a "Day in the Life" of a recruit. And to top it off we are paid a whopping $90 a month, which comes to about 50 cents an hour for a 40-hour week. But because it is closer to an 80-hour week, our pay is about 25 cents an hour, before taxes!

BEST OR WORST DUTY STATION

I really didn't have a "best" duty station, as my two-year military career was spent either training for combat or in combat. I did, however, have some enjoyable and memorable times at Fort Jackson, SC and Fort Benning, GA. So I will default to my "worst" duty station as being various locations in the Republic of South Vietnam.

The monsoon season was my introduction to the country's tropical climate. The torrential downpours occurred twice a day for about 60 minutes each time. The sky could be perfectly clear and then in a matter of minutes black clouds would roll in and the rain would come down in sheets. I could set my watch by these storms as they would appear about 12 hours apart and always one hour later each day. The skimpy rubber poncho that we carried wasn't much protection from being soaked to the gills. The searing heat and humidity that followed kept us uncomfortable for the rest of the day. The temperature was always in the 90's and it's not like we were wearing bathing suits. My heavy fatigue shirt and pants kept the heat in and after a few days were pretty ripe.

When it wasn't raining we were treading through rice paddies, swamps, and jungle streams. This guaranteed that we would be damp all day. We would take time out during our patrols and reconnaissance activities to rest and dry our boots and socks, one foot at a time. We were told to never get caught with both boots off at the same time. An extra pair of dry socks was a valuable commodity. Some advice if you are ever in this situation is to never wear underwear. Even though we were constantly getting wet the hot sun would dry our outer clothes pretty quickly, but underclothes would never dry causing all kinds of discomfort.

If these issues are not enough to qualify as the worst duty station, all the time we spent moving through the terrain, or what we commonly referred to as "humping the boonies" we were carrying everything we owned on our backs. The 25 magazines of M-16 ammunition, 10 quarts of water, five or six boxes of C-rations, four grenades, a couple of trip flares, a claymore mine, a few machine gun belts or a radio, a bed roll and some personal items added up to 70 - 80 pounds of gear. Sleeping accommodations were whatever patch of dry land we could find for the night.

Sleep if we got it came in two-hour shifts if we could endure the swarm of mosquitos that came out every night at dusk. Worse than mosquitos were the red ants that fell from above when we brushed against a low-hanging jungle vine. Their bites were worse than a bee sting. We always knew when a person in front of us had bumped into a nest when all of a sudden he dropped his gear and did the "Red Ant Dance" trying to swat away the attackers. Leeches that attached themselves to any exposed part of our bodies when we traversed a river or walked through a rice paddy were equally nasty. The first thing we did when we exited a river or rice paddy was to strip down and check our bodies for leeches. If one was found, we didn't want to pull it off as the head would stay attached to the skin. So we would douse it with insect repellant until it dislodged and if there was no repellant we burned it out with a cigarette. One night when we were on ambush patrol we were in the middle of water-filled rice paddies and were forced to sleep on top of the two-foot-wide dikes that separated the individual farms. Sometime during the night when I was asleep my leg slipped off the dike and into the rice paddy water. I awoke to a terrible itch at the bottom of my shin. When I moved my hand down to scratch it I felt that my boot lace had come undone and my pant leg was no longer stuffed into my boot. When I reached further I felt a gooey substance above the boot on my shin. Thinking it was mud from the rice paddy I grabbed it to throw it away. When it would not dislodge I realized it was a leech that had been feasting on me for quite some time and had engorged itself to become about five inches long. I ripped it out, squeezed it as hard as I could, and blood spurted all over my shirt.

Though the physical aspects are demanding the harder part is the psychological being that you have to quickly adapt to. Your simple stateside routine of driving a car, telephoning a friend, hanging on the corner, going out for a slice of pizza or watching TV is no longer available. The amazing part is how quickly you do adapt and how limited hygiene, deprived sleep and dirty clothes develops a hardness that becomes your new normal. Your mindset can be summed up by the 1965 hit song by the Animals. A number of us had small transistor radios that we could listen to the one station, Armed Forces Radio, when we were in a quiet secured area. There was one song that was played multiple times during the day. When it came on anyone with a radio sang along and all other soldiers in the area joined in. Weary soldiers in dirty fatigues singing at the top of their lungs made for a strange chorus. The song was "We Gotta Get Out of This Place." How appropriate.

These hardships were offset somewhat by the fine cuisine that we experienced. There is nothing quite like eating cold spaghetti out of a can for breakfast. Canned scrambled eggs, ham and lima beans, pork slices, turkey loaf, beans with meatballs, and beef with mashed potatoes were some of the other C-ration culinary delights that we feasted on. C-rations came in a case and included 12 individually boxed meals. The box would contain a main meal as described above along with canned fruit and a tin of crackers and cheese or a round chocolate bar. There would also be a packet of coffee with sugar and powdered cream. After a year of this I guess that is why I never complain about the taste of any meal.

And by the way, the whole time we were enjoying these activities, people were trying to kill us!

Oh well, it was only for a year.

Delicious C-Rations

Turkey Loaf – Yum!

11B10

The military has a language all of its own that is built on acronyms and numbers, and one of the first newbies learn is "MOS" - Military Occupation Specialty. In other words, what is my job? Just like in civilian life there are a wide variety of jobs available. There are truck drivers, cooks, clerks, mechanics, pilots, barbers, statisticians, computer geeks, medics, nurses, doctors, dentists and every other occupation one can think of. However, there is only one that stands out when I think of a soldier, and that one is "11B10 Light Weapons Infantryman."

For all of the armament the military has at its disposal, airplanes, warships and artillery pieces, nothing can replace the infantry soldier. The military can drop bombs from above, lob shells from offshore or fire round after round from large cannons, but the only way they can win a battle is with the "grunts" on the ground. This fact isn't unique to Vietnam, it holds true back to ancient times. I am not saying that these other weapons are not important; they are a vital part of any battle. However, no one can defeat an enemy with overwhelming fire power alone. That we did learn in Vietnam.

So what is an infantryman? It starts in basic training. For me it was at Fort Jackson, South Carolina where every soldier regardless of their MOS learns the various aspects of being an infantryman. They become proficient in firing an M-14 rifle and learn the basics of first aid, hand to hand combat and camouflage. They also become familiar with D&C (drill and ceremony), KP (kitchen police) and PT (physical training). After these eight weeks of training we advance to an additional nine weeks of AIT (advanced individual training). If you are a truck driver you learn to drive the various wheeled vehicles the Army has. If you are a cook you learn how to prepare the culinary delights that soldiers complain about. If you are an "11B10" you go to Advanced Infantry Training.

If basic training is akin to elementary school then AIT is like high school. I didn't have to go far as my AIT was at Fort Jackson as well. I knew the basics of being a soldier, but now I built upon them. I became familiar with all of the weapons in an infantryman's arsenal like the M-60 machine gun, the M-79 grenade launcher, the M-72 LAW (light anti-tank weapon) and, most importantly, my M-16 automatic rifle. We do more PT and add in obstacle courses, map reading, orienteering, forced marches, and overnight maneuvers and we quickly get the point that this is going to be a tough job.

One of the side benefits of AIT was getting some weekend passes. I guess the Army figured that after eight weeks of basic training and a few more weeks of infantry training we needed some social interaction with non-military types. I had three or four weekenders at the end of AIT where four of us would head off to Columbia, South Carolina, which was just outside the base. We'd leave after lunch on Saturday and have to be back by dinner on Sunday. But that brief 24 hour respite was just what we needed. We'd get a hotel room for $20 and then walk up and down the main street that consisted of mostly bars, pawn shops and movie theaters. The drinking age was 18 so we were able to visit many of the fine establishments. One Saturday afternoon we actually stayed in the hotel room with a case of beer to watch the Army/Navy football game. Army won 21-14, but I was actually rooting for Navy as two of my North Quincy High school teammates, Lang Willis and Paul Zambernardi, were playing for the midshipmen.

After these additional nine weeks of training most 11Bravos are off to Vietnam. However, for a select group including me, it was a 30-day leave and then an assignment to attend Combat Leadership School (CLS) at Fort Benning, Georgia. If AIT was like high school then CLS was going to college. This was a 12-week course that continued with more weapons and physical training, but added in tactics and leadership aspects to our overall knowledge. The idea was to groom us to become squad leaders for our next assignment, which would eventually be Vietnam. This is where another one of my value judgments came into play. Although it was a 12-week course we had the opportunity to drop out after 8 weeks. If I completed the full 12 weeks I would be assigned to a stateside basic training unit for three months, where I would put my newly-found leadership skills to work on raw recruits. After this three-month duty I'd be off to Vietnam as a sergeant to lead a seasoned infantry squad. If I dropped out after eight weeks it was simply off to Vietnam. My decision was purely based on how much more time I wanted to stay in the Army. If I went to Vietnam after my eight-week commitment I would have just a year left to go. If I did the full 12 weeks I would end up with 16 months left to serve. As I was headed for Vietnam anyway I figured 12 more months in the Army was better that 16. So after another 30 day leave it was off to Vietnam.

Again, one of the benefits of being in the Army is the people I met. In the case of Fort Benning it was Joe Casey and Joe Harding. Both are great guys and made the miserable time at CLS bearable and humorous. Joe Casey was from Woburn, MA and eventually settled in Alexandria, VA where I was able to visit him a few times over the years. I went to his and his girlfriend Maureen's wedding about two months after we got out of the service. Joe Harding is from North Quincy and actually did not live that far from me. He was a few years older and went to Boston College High School so that is why we never connected. I went to Joe and Jan's wedding the week after I went to Joe Casey's wedding. Even more coincidental was, after being in Vietnam for a month, a helicopter dropped in with some replacement troops, and who jumped off the chopper but Joe Harding. We were together for the next four and a half -months which was reassuring. Our moms became friends during that time, sharing letters and information as they received it from us. I lost touch with Joe for a long time, but we reconnected in 2007 at his dad's wake and we have kept in touch since.

Over the past 50 years I have always worn lapel pins or baseball caps with the insignia of the two units I served with in Vietnam, the 82nd Airborne Division and the 11th Armored Calvary Regiment. The 82nd is one of the most famous units in the history of the US military. Besides all of the regular infantry training they endure they also complete a three-week course where they jump out of airplanes to earn their paratrooper wings. When people see my 82nd insignia they immediately think I was a paratrooper. I let them know right away, "Why would anybody want to jump out of a perfectly good airplane?" So how did I get into the 82nd?

When I first landed in Vietnam as we exited the plane we were told to count off by threes. Once we were on the tarmac there were buses with corresponding numbers one to three that we hopped on. Those on bus number one were sent to the 1st Air Cavalry Division. Those on bus number two went to the 9th Infantry Division. The lucky number three bus sent its men to the 82nd. As there were no airborne assaults in Vietnam, the 82nd didn't need qualified paratroopers. More importantly, there was a combat arms manpower shortage so units were happy to get replacements of any kind.

As an aside, the term "combat arms personnel" refers to anyone who is in the infantry, armor or artillery. These are the units on the front lines that initiate contact with the enemy on a regular basis. Most people do not realize that for every combat soldier there are 5 or 6 staff that support them. This staff includes the truck drivers, clerks, cooks, supply staff, mechanics, logistics, and medical people that are usually in the rear areas. So during the Vietnam War when we had 500,000 military personnel in country there were only about 80,000 to 90,000 men assigned to combat arms units. But to be clear, anyone who was in country no matter where they were assigned was in harm's way.

The makeup of an infantry unit is identified in the standard Army Table of Organization. The 82nd Airborne is a division that is made up of four Brigades; a Brigade is made up of four Regiments; a Regiment has four Battalions; a Battalion consists of four Companies; a Company has four Platoons and each Platoon has four Squads. So when I landed in country I become a member of the 1st Squad, 4th Platoon of Charley Company which is part of the 2nd Battalion of the 505th Regiment of the 3rd Brigade of the 82nd Airborne Division. There were 10 men in the First Squad and we all became very close as our tour of duty unfolded. These were the people I relied on when things got tough and the ones I communicated with to keep my sanity. One of the unique aspects of an infantry unit is that we carry everything we own on our backs or anyplace else we can find on our bodies. Each man has a large ruck sack that civilians would call a backpack without cute little insignias. Fatigue uniforms are designed with a number of pockets. The shirt has two breast pockets and two large pouches on the bottom of the shirt. The pants have two large pockets at the thigh level and will later be popularized as "cargo pants." So what do we carry? The most important item is our M-16 automatic rifles. The M-16 weighs about 7 pounds and can be set for a semi- or fully-automatic firing. Of course we need ammunition which we carry in 25 magazines with 20 rounds in each. One thing we learn in weapons training is that we go to fully automatic sparingly. There are two reasons: one, the rifle loses all accuracy on fully automatic and two, the rifle goes through a 20-round magazine in 2 seconds. For that reason we are trained to fire in 2-3 round bursts. Our other armaments include 2 hand grenades, 2 smoke grenades, 2 hand-held parachute flares, a couple of trip flares and a claymore mine. Along with our weapons we carry 10 quarts of water in various canteens, a rubber poncho with liner, cans of c-rations that will last us for three days, and our personal hygiene products. All told we will be carrying about 70 to 80 pounds of gear wherever we go.

Not all squad members carry an M-16. One of the men is assigned an M-79 grenade launcher that is a single shot shoulder-fired weapon that fires an explosive projectile that is a little smaller than a regular hand grenade. It has a range of 300 meters and comes in handy if the enemy is dug in or behind cover. Another member of the squad carries the M-60 machine gun. The M-60 is a heavy belt-fed weapon that can fire continuously with the trigger depressed and has a range of 1,000 meters. Even though the weapon can fire continuously, like the M-16, we are trained to fire in 3-5 round bursts, which gives us plenty of cover. Another aspect of the M-60 is that the ammunition comes in 100 round belts. The M-60 gunner will have one 100 round belt locked and loaded into his weapon and carry an additional five or six belts wrapped around his body. As five or six belts can be used up quickly, seven other members of the squad will wrap two or three additional belts around their chests to give the gunner a good supply of ammo. The grenade launcher carries the extra weight of 30-40 grenades so he is spared carrying any machine gun belts. That still leaves one man unaccounted for - the radio telephone operator (RTO).

The RTO is a vital component of all infantry units. Along with his M-16 and all the other gear, he carries a 20-pound ANPRC-25 radio that is the only method of communication between the squad in the field and any support that is needed. The position is especially vital to call in fire support when engaging the enemy and for medivac helicopters to evacuate the wounded. The RTO is connected at the hip with the squad and/or platoon leaders and is in the middle of all action. Because communication is such an important part of any action the squad/platoon leaders and the RTO are prime targets. To make life even more challenging, the ANPRC has a 15-foot expandable antenna that must be engaged anytime communication is needed thus giving the enemy a better fix on the target. So at 6' 2" and 200 pounds you would think I would not be a good candidate to be an RTO. Well you would be wrong. RTO was my job the entire time I spent with the 82nd. I had learned the basics of the radio in AIT, but now I had to put it to use. All soldiers memorize the phonetic alphabet, Alpha, Bravo, Charlie, Delta.........X-ray, Yankee, Zula and I still use it to this day when I need to emphasize a specific letter. Call signs to communicate with each platoon were changed regularly and were eclectic in nature. One that I remember well was based on various brands of whiskey. The platoon signs were Cutty Sark, Jim Beam and Wild Turkey. By this time I had been promoted and was now the RTO for the company commander, Captain Tom Schwartz, and our call sign was Johnnie Walker. Captain Schwartz could have been a model for an Army recruiting poster. He was 6'3 and his 230 pounds were all muscle. A square jaw and piercing eyes completed the picture. He was a 1967 graduate of West Point and a three-year starter as defensive end on their football team. He made a career out of the Army and retired as a Four-Star General. An example of a simple communication would be: Cutty Sark Six this is Johnnie Walker Six, what is your position? Over. Johnnie Walker Six this is Cutty Sark Six we are two kilometers north of your position. Over. Cutty Sark Six this is Johnnie Walker Six stay in place. Out. Contrary to what you hear in war movies you never end a conversation with "over and out."

So that gives a brief description of how I become an infantryman and how I was outfitted. The next few stories will give a feeling for how my time was spent.

KP at Fort Benning

John and Joe Harding

John packed and ready to go

M-60 machine gun

11B10 CONTINUED (1)

No amount of training can really prepare us for what we will encounter in the field. We can do plenty of physical training, learn to apply camouflage, and go on all the long marches and night maneuvers we want, but we are still in South Carolina. We can do hours of live firing exercises, feel the concussion of explosives, and discuss tactics all we want, but we are still in Georgia. So believe me, no one can replicate the nervousness and yes, fear, as our squad of ten sits in a rice paddy on a quiet starlit night afraid to swat a mosquito because it may make a sound, knowing there could be people waiting in the dark wanting to kill us.

After landing in Vietnam my first week was spent in the rear area getting acclimated to the heat, zeroing in my M-16 and participating in more training sessions. Then one morning I got the word, "Ok cherry, it's time to go out to the field." I hop on a deuce and a half with a few other replacements and ride a couple of hours to northwest of Saigon. We pass through the outskirts of the city and marvel that it looks like any major metropolitan area in the states. There are high rise buildings, sidewalks teeming with people and streets clogged with traffic. However, once outside the city limits the landscape changes quickly. Rice paddies stretch for miles and everywhere we look there are dilapidated shacks that people call homes. Building materials include clumps of thatched palm leaves for roofs, cardboard boxes nailed to roughly-cut tree limbs to form walls, and flattened beer cans glued to the cardboard for aesthetics. I am definitely not in Quincy anymore.

Our destination is a firebase where I get indoctrinated into what I can expect for the next year. A firebase is a somewhat fortified area that includes stationary artillery pieces whose function is to provide fire support for troops in the field. As a secondary objective the bases serve as protection for strategic areas like the junction of major roads or bridges over river crossings. For protection the bases are ringed with concertina wire which is metal wire with razor sharp barbs spaced every six inches along the strands. There are also a number of sand-bagged bunkers that line the perimeter and are manned 24 hours a day. The bunkers are simple structures put together by layering sandbags in a square and laying metal roofing material across the top. There are a few openings for ventilation and a place to position an M-60 machine gun on the roof. The bunkers not only provide more protection when we are on guard duty, but also give us a more comfortable place to sleep.

I jump off the truck and am introduced to my squad. As a newbie they fill me in on what I am supposed to do. Basically it is to listen to the people who have been there for a while and don't do anything stupid.

On my first day in the field I pull guard duty on one of the bunkers. This means I do two hour shifts behind the M-60 watching the countryside and then have two hours where I can rest or sleep. Not bad duty. However, the next day I find out that my squad will be going out on an ambush patrol that night. Now it hits me that this is all real. The day goes by slowly as I wonder what the night will bring. As an infantryman I assume that I will be sloshing through the rice paddies on our way to the ambush position. We saddle up at dusk and to my surprise we walk just a few meters to a dock along the Saigon River where our firebase is located. There are two large Boston Whalers with mounted M-60 machine guns waiting for us. We load on to these boats and motor down river to our ambush site. It's a silent journey as the open rice paddies slowly disappear into triple canopy jungle. Even though the sun is out, tall trees and jungle vines cover us in darkness. We are a few miles into our trip when we are hit with enemy small arms fire. It is amazing how fast one reacts to being shot at. The adrenalin kicks in and I immediately respond with my own fire. The battle lasts just a few minutes and the patrol leader orders the boats to land on the bank of the river so that we can pursue our attackers. It is a futile attempt as the vegetation is so thick we can't move and there is no field of vision. The decision is made to stay there for the night so we quickly unload as the boats head back to the firebase. We are now a few miles from where we were supposed to land in an unfamiliar place with no dry area to settle into. I position myself against a tree with my boots in the water and am told that I will be on guard for the next two hours with another soldier while the rest of the squad sleeps. The night is eerily quiet even with the constant noise of jungle insects. The time goes by slowly as I look into the darkness wondering what is out there. Two hours later I get a tap on the shoulder telling me I am relieved and can catch some shut eye. There is no way I am going to sleep and I stay awake the rest of the night waiting for something to happen. I will learn that there will be many nights like this where we are ready for anything, but nothing occurs. Eventually the sun rises and two boats appear on the horizon to take us back to the firebase. I am relieved that I made it through my first contact, but all I can think of is, "I've got 12 more months of this. How am I going to make it?"

Typical village

Local villagers

Easy day at our bunker

11B10 CONTINUED (2)

I am assigned to the 82nd for the next five months. A routine is established. We spend three days in the firebase doing recon sweeps of the area during the day and setting up ambush patrols at night and then three days in the "boonies" doing the same, but living totally under the stars. As we have three platoons in Charley Company, we rotate so that one platoon stays back to pull security at the firebase at night while the other two are out on ambush patrol. I soon learn that one night out of six being able to sleep on a cot in a sandbagged bunker is like a night at the Ritz.

The recon sweeps take us through the local landscape looking for signs of enemy activity. As we are in an agricultural area with large rice paddies and a number of small villages the enemy is the Viet Cong (VC). We have no idea what the enemy looks like as they blend in with the local population. They can even be the kindly farmer you see sloshing behind a water buffalo tilling the soil during the day who turns into a VC squad leader at night. The mission is made even harder as there are strict orders of when we can initiate fire. During the daylight no one fires unless fired upon.

One of our recon patrols brought me to a large empty village that actually had some buildings made out of concrete and stucco. The difference from other villages I had encountered were the buildings were bombed out shells. Earlier in the day it was reported that there was enemy fire from this village. My platoon was tasked with clearing the area to ensure no Viet Cong soldiers were still around. Each building was searched and various pieces of enemy equipment was found. I was with the squad leader, Arthur Ring from Providence, when the platoon sergeant said he thought he saw some movement outside of one of the buildings. There was a large hole in the ground with a thatch covered top that was used to store rice. In many instances these storage areas were openings for Viet Cong tunnels. The sergeant thought he saw someone jump into this hole so he positioned Art and I on each side of a doorway in one of the buildings covering the area with our M-16's at the ready.

The platoon sergeant indicated that he would move to the side of the building, run across the area and drop a hand grenade into the storage hole. When the grenade went off Art and I were to come out of the building firing at the entrance. While the platoon sergeant made his way around the building Art I were concentrating on the area in front of us. Art looked at me and said, "Hey, Big John, this is just like in the movies." With that we both broke out laughing and only stopped when we heard a grenade explode. We quickly whirled out of the doorway with M-16's blazing and filled the hole with lead. When the dust settled we looked inside the storage bin and found it was empty except for a few handfuls of rice. So much for my John Wayne moment.

The ambush patrols are like what I described in the previous story. We usually go out in squad size units stripped of all our extraneous gear except our weapons, ammunition and rubber ponchos. Depending on how far we have to go, we will form up an hour or so before dusk. Unlike my first few weeks with the luxury of being ferried to the ambush sites via light boats, the normal mode of transportation for the infantryman is our legs. We head out with 10 men in a line with five to ten yards between each soldier. We are careful never to bunch up in open spaces and try to stay off the well-traveled paths. As a result, much of our journey is spent walking through rice paddies and fording small streams. Before we even get to the ambush site we are soaking wet and uncomfortable.

And it is not like we can set up anywhere we want. Before we leave the firebase the squad leader is given specific coordinates where our squad will position themselves for the night. This is important as there will be other units spread out at sites across the area and the last thing anyone wants to see happen is friendlies firing on friendlies. The other reason for being given specific coordinates is to have the artillery and/or mortar units get a true fix on positions in order to provide fire support if needed. We try to reach our ambush site as close to dark as possible to cloak our position. If we get there too early the standard procedure is to walk past the actual site and pretend to set up our ambush a mile away. We then wait until dark and move back to the appointed site. Once we get to the site we usually set up in what was called the traditional Lshaped ambush. It is simply two five-man units set up perpendicular to each other to cover two of our flanks. We then quickly set up claymore mines which are command-detonated explosive devices that fire off hundreds of ball bearings in a 30-degree arc. Once we are all positioned a guard/sleep rotation is established. Usually everyone stays awake until 2100 or 2200 hours and then two men at a time are designated to be awake while the others try to get some sleep. Every hour a new man takes over. So we rarely get more than two hours of sleep at any one time.

This is when it gets scary. I am one of the two on guard in the middle of the night. There is no sound except for the quiet noise made by buzzing insects. As we are miles from any light source a moonless night exposes the billions of stars in the sky. If I were some place different it would be a calming and pleasant experience. However, I am anxious and scared. I don't know what is out there and every foreign sound is magnified in my brain as something sinister. I am constantly moving my eyes because if they stay transfixed on something I will swear that something moved. Years later I reflect on this experience and realize how profound it was. I am barely out of high school sitting in a rice paddy 10,000 miles from home with nine other guys whose mission is to literally kill other people. Think about that.

Dawn is approaching and the cool night air is replaced by the searing heat of the sunrise that results in an eerie scene of ground fog covering the rice paddies. The squad awakes and puts their gear together. As is the case for many of the nights, there were no enemy encounters. We are relieved and happy that we are one day closer to going home.

Rice paddy

Bombed out village

Captured AK-47 and
RPG rounds

John with Arthur Ring

That's Joe Harding on the right,
Arthur Ring standing,
and John on the left

11B10 CONTINUED (3)

So that gives an idea of what the routine of an infantry soldier is. But the three days at the firebase and then three days in the boonies quickly changes to two days at the firebase and four days in the boonies. Then we go to one day at the firebase and six or seven days in the boonies. And then there are times when we go three or four weeks straight in the boonies. It is physically demanding and mentally fatiguing. The days seem longer than 24 hours and there are more than seven days in a week. The short periods where our adrenalin rises are followed by longer periods of boredom. We are carrying around 70 pounds of gear as we slosh through the rice paddies and because it is monsoon season we are constantly soaking wet. I remember one time we had to traverse a swamp to get to an open area for choppers to pick us up. It looked simple. We were on a small area of dry land and the pickup point was just 100 yards away. There were about 90 of us and we started out one man at a time keeping about 10 yards between us. We didn't want to have too many men in the water at the same time in case the enemy was waiting in ambush. This simple maneuver turned complicated when the first few men started sinking up to their thighs in mud. Every step was a physical chore and we literally had to pull our legs out of the mud each time we moved. After about 10 guys were in the water we needed to form a second line. Even with that it took us five hours to go that short distance.

While legs are our main mode of transportation, there is an alternate way of getting from one place to another that is faster and exciting, but definitely more dangerous. My first air assault via a Huey helicopter would be fun and exhilarating if we were at an amusement park. However, flying at treetop level at over 100 miles per hour to minimize the time the enemy can focus in and shoot can be somewhat unnerving. I did 20 or 30 of these air assaults. The assault team consists of five or six choppers each with six infantrymen on board. The choppers come into the landing zone fast and low. There are two door gunners behind their M-60 machine guns laying down protective fire. The chopper barely touches ground as the six soldiers jump out and the bird rises quickly to leave the area. Our first reaction when we hit the ground is to move as quickly as possible away from the helicopter. The reasoning is, if there are enemy soldiers nearby, they will opt to target the chopper rather than an individual soldier. After that joy ride I return to who I am, a regular "ground pounder."

I rode in Huey's dozens of more times in addition to the air assaults. There were many occasions where my platoon/company had to reposition to areas to far away to travel by foot. These were more relaxing trips and actually gave me an entertaining view of the landscape. Geographically, Vietnam is a beautiful country. The lush green vegetation framed by the clear blue sky would give you a soothing feeling if you didn't wonder what was lurking below.

I look forward to the every-third-day resupply helicopter that brings us a new selection of c-rations, water to fill our canteens and hopefully a letter from home. A simple pleasure is dividing up the c-ration cases with my squad members.

A c-ration case would consist of a dozen small boxes each containing canned goods that would provide a full meal. There would be a main item like spaghetti, pork slices, ham and lima beans or beef stew along with a small can containing crackers and cheese, chocolate bars or a piece of cake. The most recognizable food is a can of fruit cocktail, sliced pears or peaches. Dividing up the boxes is based on seniority and we know we are short-timers if we are able to choose "peaches and pound cake." Later in my tour we are introduced to LRRP (Long Range Recon Patrol) rations. These are freeze dried offerings that you just add hot water to come up with a hot meal. The benefit is that they are lighter and more compact to carry. Every once in a while a chopper leaves five cases of beer and five cases of soda with a few large blocks of ice. Each man in the company takes one beer and one soda and chips off some ice into his canteen cup. Fine champagne never tasted so good. I try to fill up my time, but the reality is that there is not much I can do but wait it out, stay focused, and dream about going home.

The Vietnam War brought an added feature to infantry strategy never seen before: the helicopter. All of a sudden whole units could move faster and farther than ever before, and there was an entirely new method of delivering fire power that was outright scary. Let's go through some different varieties of helicopters that supported our ground troops.

The **CH-47 Chinook** was a large clumsy looking helicopter with two rotating blades. It was the Allied Moving Van of the Army. It had a back door ramp where several light vehicles could easily drive inside the body. Or it could accommodate a platoon-size complement of infantrymen (40) with all their gear. It even had a cargo hook system that could carry artillery pieces from its underbelly. This allowed the Army to relocate an entire company to a new sector in a very short time, and gave strategists more flexibility.

The **OH-6 LOACH** (Light Observation and Command Helicopter) was a small two-man helicopter present at battle sites to forward information to troops on the ground. The two crewmen were the pilot and an observer (who in many cases was a battalion commander) who could assess movement better from a 1,000-foot level than from right on the ground.

If the Chinook was the Allied Moving Van of the Army then the **AH-1 Cobra** gunship was a combination of a Ferrari and Clint Eastwood. It was sleek, powerful, and a total badass and like an automobile, it came with options. In the Cobra's case there were two armament designs. One carried two rocket launcher pods, one on each side. The other carried two mini guns, again one on each side. The rocket launchers had a supply of 19 rockets apiece and were best used in heavily- wooded areas or against bunker complexes. However, the weapon of choice was the mini gun. This weapon had a rotating set of six barrels firing M-14 ammunition at the rate of 3000 rounds per minute. Because of the rotating barrels there was less of a chance of overheating compared to having an M-16 on automatic fire. The nickname of the Cobra was "the snake." While an obvious nickname, another version of how the nickname came about was the visual effect of firing its mini guns at night. Firing from 1,000 feet above a target especially at night doesn't lend itself to accuracy. To assist the pilot in walking in his fire to the target the ammunition belts feeding the mini guns had a tracer round every fifth bullet. The tracer round burned bright red as it headed for its target. Because the Cobra was firing 3000 rounds a minute, even with only every fifth round being a tracer it looked like a straight line of red heading to the ground. As the pilot adjusted his weapon to fire in one direction or another the red line wiggled up and down like a snake slithering through the grass. Thus another reason for the moniker, "the snake."

The workhorse, and most indispensable chopper, was the **UH-1 Huey Slick.** This is probably the most recognizable helicopter in the world and it served multiple purposes. Its foremost mission was to move infantry units quickly from one site to another. Sometimes it was used just to reposition units which was pretty uneventful. But there were many times that the Huey carried six soldiers into a hot landing zone knowing that there was a good possibility that there would be enemy contact. The Huey crew consisted of a pilot and co-pilot as well as two door gunners who manned M-60 machine guns. At first we were a little jealous of these door gunners. They didn't have to hump the boonies, and because the choppers were stationed in a rear area they were safe on the ground, had clean fatigues, slept on a real bed and had hot meals and hot showers. But we eventually realized that theirs was the most dangerous job in the world. Statistics show that there were just over 7,000 Huey helicopters deployed in Vietnam and over 3,300, almost half, were shot down or crashed with a loss of almost 5,000 men. I think I was better off as a grunt. The Huey was also the ship that brought in our re-supplies, but their most important job was to extract the wounded from the battlefield and fly them back to the rear area hospitals. These medivac missions were highly dangerous because many times they occurred in the middle of a battle. With enemy fire concentrated on them, the Huey pilots knew that the difference between a wounded man living or dying was how fast they could get in and get them out. As a final line on its resume, the Huey could be outfitted with two mini guns or rocket launchers, much like the Cobra, and act as a pure hunter. I am glad they were on our side.

Staying with air power there were some fixed wing aircraft that supported ground troops in a big way.

The **F-4 Phantom** was a large fighter/bomber that flew at 1,500 miles per hour and carried up to 18,000 pounds of bombs. They were also armed with air-to-air missiles and a 20-millimeter cannon. Though air to air combat was not prevalent in Vietnam the F-4s did manage to shoot down over 100 Russian MiGs assigned to the North Vietnam Air Force. Their value to infantry support was their ability to drop a large amount of ordinance into a confined space usually on bunker and tunnel complexes. I witnessed a few occasions where the Phantom-4s were effective without dropping bombs. One plane swooped in over a bunker complex and dropped two fifty-five-gallon drums of JP-4 jet fuel with a detonator and then watched as it created a fireball on the ground. The fireball sucked all of the oxygen out of the air. Anyone in a tunnel or bunker began to gasp for air and ran out of the confined space. As they exited their underground protection a second Phantom-4 swooped in with its 20-millimeter cannons blazing.

The **B-52 Stratofortress** is the largest bomber in the world, carrying a bomb payload of 70,000 pounds. It has a range of 8,000 miles and can fly at a height of 50,000 feet. During the Vietnam War US planes dropped over 7.5 million tons of bombs with over half from B-52s. For security purposes the B-52's were based on the island of Guam over 2,600 miles from Vietnam. So for each bombing mission these planes would have about a 10-hour round trip flight. When I was with the 11th Armored Cav I witnessed one B-52 mission. All B-52 missions had the code name Arc Light. We were told beforehand that an Arc Light mission would drop its payload on a hilly crest at precisely 1400 hours. We were in our armored vehicles a few miles from the attack zone ready to move in after the drop. At exactly 1400 I started to hear a slight buzzing in the air. The day was cloudless, but I could not see any aircraft in the sky. The buzzing increased its intensity to an almost deafening pitch. A few seconds after the buzzing ceased the ground around us shook as violently as an earthquake. Anything on our vehicles that was not secured flew into the air. Then the sound of the explosion reached us and lasted for a minute as the last bomb hit the ground. We then moved to the drop zone to assess the damage and found that there was no enemy activity, but the destruction of the forested area was immense. To think of the destructive power of one plane was sobering.

Finally, there was **Puff the Magic Dragon** - no, not the mythical monster made famous by Peter, Paul, and Mary, but the **AC-47 Spooky Gunship**. The A-47 was a fixed wing propeller-driven plane that was outfitted with three mini guns on the left side. The gunship circled an area providing maximum fire support to troops on the ground. It fired up to 6,000 rounds a minute, enough to cover every square foot of a football field in under 60 seconds. The smoke emitting from the mini guns during daylight or the lines of red tracers at night gave the impression of a fire-breathing dragon.

So that gives an idea of what being an 11Bravo was like. However, Vietnam wasn't all combat. There were a few instances where I actually felt like I was back at home even though I was 10,000 miles away.

Chinook carrying a payload

OH-6 LOACH   Huey bringing resupply

WHO THOUGHT THIS WAS A GOOD IDEA?

It's 0600 and the First Squad, Fourth Platoon, Charlie Company, Second Battalion, 505th Regiment, Third Brigade of the 82nd Airborne Division is trudging back to our base camp after our nightly ambush patrol. For the past three months we have been conducting reconnaissance in force during the day and setting up ambush sites at night. We are all tired, hungry, and dirty and are looking forward to some breakfast and sleep.

But first I need to go through my bathing ritual. Each man carries 10 quarts of water that has to last him for three days. I pour a quart of water from one of my canteens into my steel helmet. I proceed to wash my hands, face, armpits, crotch and feet using that precious quart of water. That is as clean as I will be for the rest of the day. Then it is time for breakfast. I open one of the five or six C-ration boxes that I carry in my ruck sack. I think I will do spaghetti this morning. As cold spaghetti is not really appetizing for breakfast I decide to heat it up. Where is the microwave? Oh yeah, it hasn't been invented yet. So I go to Plan B. I take an empty C-ration can, cut the lid off, punch a few holes in the side with a can opener and pop in a two-inch blue heating tab. The tab lasts for four or five minutes and gives off some powerful heat. I then put the can of spaghetti on top of the heating can, stir occasionally, and before I know it have a meal that will rival any fine dining establishment in the area.

It is getting to be around 0700 and today we are expecting our every third day visit by two Huey helicopters that will resupply us with ammo, water, food and mail in that priority. For those of us who have the pleasure of a one year all- expense paid trip to exotic Southeast Asia, the eerie sound and site of an incoming chopper will stay with us for life. The distinctive whoop, whoop, whoop sound of the blades gets louder and louder as it nears your position. Someone will pop a red, yellow, or purple smoke grenade to mark the landing zone. The procedure is for the pilot to identify the color of the smoke grenade to ensure he is in the right place. You don't want the person on the ground identifying what color they just popped. If the enemy has somehow monitored our radio transmission they could pop a like color to lure the pilot to the wrong landing zone. As an example I would pop a red smoke grenade and radio the pilot "smoke has been popped." The pilot returns with "I see red smoke." Even if the enemy is listening and pops a similar color it would be obvious that the second smoke was from the wrong source. The pilot comes in fast and everything and everyone in the area gets covered with dust from the rotating blades. We unload the aircraft as quickly as possible because choppers are sitting ducks on the ground. Today the pilots stay on the ground a little longer as our platoon leader has informed us that the First Squad is going on "Stand Down."

Military leaders are tasked with many logistical, strategic, political, and human resource challenges. One challenge that has been with the military since the beginning of time is how to maintain soldier morale. Someone in Vietnam decided, "Hey let's take a squad that has been in the field for a couple of months, fly them back to the rear area, and give them a 24-hour pass to Saigon." What could possibly go wrong? So our 10-man squad loads into the two Huey's and 40 minutes later we land at Ton Son Nhut Air Base which borders Saigon. We get a chance for a real shower, a clean set of fatigues, and an actual hot meal. We are able to draw out $100 from our Military Bank account, jump in a deuce and a half, and are whisked off to downtown Saigon. The driver lets us off in front of the USO Club and the sergeant with him tells us in no uncertain terms that we are to be back in front of the club no later than 0800 the next morning. If we are not there we will be considered AWOL with all of the relevant punishments to follow. We enter the USO club and get a quick meal. A hamburger with French fries never tasted so good. We then check with one of the workers to find out where we might stay for the evening. The USO workers tell us there are two or three very nice hotels that cater to Americans, so we have them make reservations for us.

So here we are - 10 guys who have been out in the field for the last three months not only fighting the enemy, but enduring the elements, sleeping on the ground, making friends with all kinds of bugs, eating C-rations and not having a cold beer.

Saigon is a cosmopolitan city with wide avenues, classic architecture, high rise office buildings, fabulous restaurants, world-renowned religious temples and museums and hundreds of seedy bars. If you guessed we spent our time at the museums or admiring the architecture,

Religious Temple, Saigon

you'd be wrong. Of course we headed straight for the seedy bars. On our way out of the USO we encountered a rather nasty MP who for some reason did not like our raucous behavior. I think I may have questioned his dietary habits, as he was extremely rotund.

Off we went as a group hitting one bar after another. As we were walking down one of the large avenues we encountered a Vietnamese person who offered to do some money exchanging. We carry Military Payment Certificates (MPC) which are like green backs but with different scenes on the bills. The going exchange rate was one dollar in MPC for 118 Vietnamese piasters. This fine gentleman offered one of our squad members 1500 piasters for $10 MPC, an almost 50% return on investment. Even though this kind of transaction was totally forbidden by the military, he jumped at the chance. And guess what? The fine Vietnamese fellow took the $10 of MPC, palmed the roll of 1500 piasters, gave our fellow squad member a roll of about 100 piasters and scooted off before anyone realized it.

Stung by this bait and switch we agreed not to partake in any other transactions with the local people. That was until another fine gentleman noticed a yellow box stuffed into my fatigue pants pocket. When we first arrived at the USO I had purchased a Kodak Instamatic camera for $10, took the camera out of the box, placed it in my fatigue shirt pocket, and put the empty box in my pants pocket. This fine gentleman offered me 1500 piasters as he pointed to the yellow box, not knowing that it was empty. Realizing this new transaction would make up for our friend's previous loss I jumped at it. He gave me the 1500 piasters and I gave him the empty box and hustled away. In the meantime my fellow squad members had moved on from me not realizing what I was doing. When the fine gentleman finally realized what had happened I was making my getaway down the street. Unfortunately, the rest of my squad members were further down than I realized and I hastened my effort to get to them. All of a sudden a small car pulled up beside me and four small but menacing-looking Vietnamese exited and one was holding the yellow box. They indicated their wish that I return the 1500 piasters which I refused. As they came closer I noticed my squad members about 50 yards away and yelled "Airborne." They saw me encountering the four Vietnamese and in unison nine soldiers charged towards them. Needless to say the four menacing Vietnamese jumped in their car and sped away.

As this altercation did not hinder our attempts to visit as many seedy bars as possible, the afternoon progressed as planned. I can't tell you how many beers we had, but we were making up for three months lost time. We had agreed that if we were separated we would meet at the USO at a certain time before heading to our hotel. Of course we got separated and at the appointed time I and another squad member headed to the USO Club. We were just about to enter the Club when the small car with the four Vietnamese pulled to the curb, got out and started arguing with me again. This was witnessed by the portly MP who I had harassed earlier in the day, and after he shooed the four Vietnamese off he called for an MP jeep. I thought that he was going to send the jeep after the four in the car, but to my surprise he told the MPs in the jeep to lock me up. I got in the jeep thinking that my time in Vietnam was just about to get worse as I was going to miss the pickup the next morning. That is when my faith in humanity was restored. The MPs in the jeep asked what was going on and I told them of my misadventures. They both started laughing, asked what hotel I was staying at, dropped me off there, and said good luck for the rest of my tour.

Well, the night didn't end there. Our squad was reunited so we went to the rooftop bar where we ordered drink after drink, danced with beautiful bar girls, and got very little sleep. The next morning we made sure that all of us showed up at the USO club at the proper time. We all were hung over and sleep deprived as the deuce and a half picked us up. An hour later we were in a helicopter on our way back to the battlefield much worse for wear.

To the military brass, I would say we had a great time, "but who thought this was a good idea?"

1st Squad,
4th Platoon,
Charlie Company,
82nd Airborne

The infamous
"yellow box"
in pants pocket

REST AND RECUPERATION

Even better than a "stand down" was Rest and Recuperation, or R and R. The military thinks of everything. In the middle of a war they find a way to give a soldier something to look forward to other than going home. While I am sitting in a rice paddy constantly thinking how nice it would be to be lying on a white sandy beach or touring an exotic city with a beautiful girl, the powers that be have just the solution. Let's send him on R and R.

R and R was basically a one-week vacation that we received in the middle of our one-year tour of duty in Vietnam. It was another surreal adventure. One day we are in the field dirty and tired and 24 hours later we are on a plane to Sydney, Australia or some other exotic land. That's what happened to me after about five months in country.

We usually do not get the opportunity to go on an R and R until we have been in Vietnam for seven or eight months. Every unit gets an allotment of places to go and they are assigned on a seniority basis. Even though I was in country for only five months I was actually one of the senior members of my company. So one day our company got notice that we had an allotment of R and R's. I was told I had first choice if I wanted one. I contemplated if I wanted to wait a few more months when my tour of duty was closer to ending, but decided to go ahead and take it then.

There were a variety of places to choose from: Tokyo, Singapore, Bangkok, Taipei, Hong Kong, Manilla, Seoul, Sydney and Honolulu. Honolulu was pretty much reserved for married guys so that they could rendezvous with their wives. The most desired place was Sydney as it was the most reminiscent of the States. I was lucky and was headed to Australia.

I hop on a chopper early one morning and fly back to our rear area where I get a real shower and hot food. I am told the maximum I can take out of my bank account is $500 and that amount will be more than enough for my time in Sydney. I do have to go to the PX to buy a polo shirt, slacks, and a pair of loafers as Sydney is the only R and R destination that does not allow American GIs to visit in their fatigues.

The next morning I am on a commercial jet for the eight-hour flight.

On the flight we are given a package of information on the dos and don'ts of our vacation as well as recommendations for hotels and things to do. By the time we land I have chosen my hotel, "The Gazebo", and have planned some of my itinerary. After touching down we are herded into a large hangar to meet with hotel representatives who will ferry us to downtown. But before we leave we need civilian clothes as all I have are the shirt and slacks I bought at the PX. Again, the Army thinks of everything. Inside the hangar is what looks like a large department store. There are racks of pants, shirts, sport coats and ties that I can rent for the week. I pick out four shirts, two pair of pants, two sports coats, a belt and three ties for $40, and then buy a half dozen pair of socks and underwear.

I take the shuttle and check in at The Gazebo, a 20-story luxury hotel with a cylindrical shape. I have a room on one of the top floors with a balcony overlooking Sydney Harbor and a clear view of the iconic Sydney Opera House, with its billowing sails, which is still under construction. It's been a whirlwind 48 hours and I am tempted to just get between the sheets and go to sleep. But it is early evening and I do not want to waste a minute of my time here.

I put on a sport coat and tie and head out for the evening. Remember, I am still only 20 years old and the only time I had ever worn a suit and tie was for special occasions. So here I was walking the streets like I was some young businessman heading home after a tough day at the office. I was content to just walk the streets and take in the sights. I hit some of the pubs, play pool with a few of the lads, and think this is what it will be like when I get home in seven months.

Each day I sleep late catching up on the last five months. I take long walks exploring the city, visiting museums, touring the zoo, and talking to the locals who love the American GIs. I even go to a performance of "Hair" the controversial rock musical of the time. The evenings are spent at King's Cross, the night club zone of the city, where I get together with other soldiers on R and R to drink, dance, and talk to the local girls. Every night is fun and I hope it will never end. But the six days fly by and before I know it I am on a plane headed back to Vietnam. I have had a taste of what the real world will be like in seven months, but now it is back to the current reality of finishing out my tour in one piece. Like a week earlier but reversed, I go from sleeping in a comfy hotel to back under the stars in a rice paddy. Was it worth it? Hell yes, and guess what? I will get to do it all over again five months later!

Yes, two R and R's. I had been in country for about ten months and was now with the 11th Armored Cavalry Regiment. One day the Commanding Officer came up to me and said, "Hey John, we have some allotments for R and R and I see you haven't had one." It turned out the Army efficiency wasn't as tight when it came to tracking who went on R and R. There was a slot to go to Sydney that I jumped on. Going for a second time was even more fun as I knew the lay of the land and all the

logistics. Even better it was the first week in February. Remember, this is the Southern Hemisphere so the weather was comparable to August in Quincy. Besides the familiar haunts that I had discovered on my first trip I spent a lot of time on Bondi Beach, one of the most beautiful beaches in the world. Again, the 6 days flew by, but on returning to Vietnam I knew I was much closer to coming home.

Gazebo Hotel
Sydney, Australia

A bit of America down under

Sydney Opera House from The Gazebo

Bondi Beach

HERE COMES THE CAVALRY

When I return from my first R and R the next thing I find out is that the 82nd is going back to the states, but only those with six months or more in country qualify to return home. I have about five and a half months in so I am being re-assigned to another unit to finish out my tour. I am leaving the infantry and going to the 11th Armored Cavalry Regiment where I'll be riding on an Armored Cavalry Assault Vehicle (ACAV). It would have been nice to go home safe and sound, but the downside would have been spending a full year pulling stateside duty to finish out my military commitment. By completing the final six and a half months of my tour in Vietnam I get an early discharge and then I can get on with my life. In the end it worked out ok.

The 11th Cavalry had been in Vietnam since 1966 and was one of the last units to leave in 1972. Its nickname is the Black Horse, and its shoulder patch is that of a black stallion rising on its hind legs on a background of red. It is an historic unit formed in the early 1900s when members actually rode on horseback. The mode of transportation is a little different now. The regiment is made up of three squadrons each consisting of three units called Troops and one unit called a Tank Company. The typical Troop has 20 M-113 ACAVs while the Tank Company is outfitted with six M-551 Sheridan Tanks. The ACAV is a 12-ton boxy vehicle with three-inch armored walls and moves on tracks instead of wheels. There is a four-man crew: a driver in a compartment in the front of the vehicle, two gunners who ride on the back side of the track behind their M-60 machine guns, and a track commander who rides on top of the vehicle in a cupola behind a 50-caliber machine gun. The vehicle looks clumsy, but is actually fairly fast and agile with a lot of fire power. The M-551 Sheridan is your traditional tank with a rotating turret that fires a 152mm cannon round. The 15-ton vehicle is also armed with two 50-caliber machine guns and is quite a formidable weapon.

The main luxury of being in an Armor unit versus the infantry is no more humping through the boonies. Our ACAV can traverse all kinds of terrain and store all our gear inside its hollow shell. The track holds all of our munitions, food rations, and water as well as folding cots to sleep on. We even have a portable shower bag that we can hang off the top of our track. Water held in a five-gallon jerry can warmed by the sun is just enough to get us cleaned and refreshed and makes life in the jungle almost bearable. The extra storage also gives us the ability to be a little more creative with our dining habits. One time I bought a 50-pound bag of rice from a local villager and treated my track mates to hot boiled rice every night. I'd even cut up some of the C-Ration ham or pork slices and mix them with the rice to enhance the flavor. What a life, except it came with one big trade off; we were in constant contact with the enemy.

Our area of operation was on the Cambodian border in fairly isolated places called the Iron Triangle and the Parrots Beak where a large part of the land was designated a free fire zone. In other words, anyone spotted in the area was not a friendly. In May of 1970 the 11th Cavalry Regiment led the infamous invasion of Cambodia to dismantle the NVA supply route commonly referred to as the Ho Chi Minh Trail. This was the last main battle of the Vietnam War and the 11th Cav was awarded numerous citations for its heroic efforts. Unfortunately, they absorbed a number of casualties, but luckily for me, I had left country about three weeks prior to the invasion. Even though the official invasion didn't begin until May, because we were so close to the border, we had many unofficial incursions into Cambodia prior to that time.

My MOS is still 11B10 and it is interesting that even though I am in a mechanized unit the experience and tactics are very similar to the infantry. We still conduct recon during the day. But instead of trudging through rice paddies and triple canopy jungle our vehicle takes us over solid hilly terrain or through enormous rubber tree plantations. Like in the infantry we still set up ambush sites at night, but we are atop our ACAV instead of lying on the ground. The rubber tree plantations are interesting. Trees 70-80 feet high set up in rows like cornfields go for miles upon miles. If we look straight down a row we can see to the horizon. Turn 45 degrees and our vision is totally blocked out by what looks like a wall of wood. We spent some time in a Michelin rubber plantation that was pretty much abandoned and spotted some of the old mansions that were now bombed out shells. Besides everything else we carried, we always kept a large can of bug spray handy. The rubber trees were about 15 feet apart, just wide enough to drive an ACAV through. There were also these large spiders that had legs about a foot long that weaved their webs from tree to tree. We would drive through the webs and the next thing we knew something out of a sci-fi movie was crawling across the top of our vehicle. A good dose of bug spray usually took care of these scary creatures.

Even though our ACAV could traverse the varied landscapes we were still reliant on regular roads to move quickly from one area to another. Outside of the major cities all roads in Vietnam were just hard packed earth. This is where we had to pay special attention to keeping in line with the vehicle in front of us. It was called tracking. The lead vehicle in our movement would set the pace and drive in a straight line down the road leaving imprints of their tracks on the hard-packed ground. The vehicles that followed needed to stay in line and roll over the same imprints. The reason for this was that at night the enemy placed explosive mines in the roads. If an ACAV ran over a mine, at a minimum a track would be blown off, temporarily disabling the vehicle. Larger mines would do much more damage. It seemed like a cavalier way of doing business, but it was an expedient way to get to our next position, until we ran over a mine. When that happened all vehicles came to a stop and we sent out a detail to sweep for mines over the next mile or two. This was a time-consuming task as we were limited in how much area we could cover. We used a metal detector, not unlike the kind people use on the beach hunting for loose change and jewelry. However, in this case the treasure was more important than finding a rusted beer can. If we did find another mine we just blew it in place. There was no value in trying to dig it up. If the road checked out for a mile or so it was back on the vehicles heading to our next destination. What about the disabled ACAV? One thing about a mechanized unit is they have to be self-sufficient. We had a wheeled vehicle traveling with us that carried spare parts and that could fabricate all kinds of metals. Sometimes a damaged vehicle could be fixed on the spot. If the damage was more serious we would leave a detachment to stay with the vehicle until it could be fixed and move on.

I was never on a track that ran over a mine, but I did come close once. Our ACAV was towing a Water Buffalo, not the animal kind, but a wheeled container that carried water. As this container was not as wide as our ACAV it did not track with our imprints. I guess the enemy had miscalculated in setting up the mine the previous night and positioned it closer to the middle of the road. Our ACAV passed over, but the Water Buffalo ran right over the mine. The next thing I hear is an explosion. I look up into the air and there is a large-wheeled container flying over my head dousing our vehicle in water.

As I mentioned, even though I am with a mechanized unit the characteristics of the infantry are still there. We no longer pull duty at a firebase because our unit is a traveling firebase. Wherever we move our troop sets up a night defensive position with our ACAVs acting as bunkers and our perimeters covered with trip flares and claymore mines. There are occasions when I still must dismount our vehicle and move through the ground to complete a mission. At night we still send out ambush patrols, but instead of lying in a rice paddy we sit on our ACAVs.

With the 82nd I was assigned to Charley Company, and now with the 11th Cav the name of my unit is F Troop. Those of a certain age will remember the TV show called F Troop about a bumbling horse cavalry military post during the Wild West era. My F Troop is nothing like that. We are a well-oiled fighting machine with great leadership and constant engagement of the enemy. As I mentioned, the 11th Cav is an historic unit and one of its Vietnam Regimental Commanders is Colonel George S. Patton IV, the son of the World War II hero. From all accounts he was much like his father as a military tactician and leader. He would often leave his command helicopter and jump on an ACAV to lead a battle directly from the ground. He was highly decorated for his actions in Vietnam with two Silver Stars, the Distinguished Flying Cross, and the Purple Heart. The motto of the 11th Cav under his leadership was "Find the Bastards, then pile on." And that we did.

We were in constant contact with the enemy and there were times when we not only engaged them on a daily basis, but for multiple times in a 24-hour period. Our superior fire power was an obvious advantage, but over the course of my six and a half months with the 11th Cav we still lost 8 soldiers from F Troop. One of those losses was Sergeant Rob Raines from Indiana. We were set up in our night defensive position when an enemy attack began with mortars and rockets followed by small arms fire. As was normal we had set up a command tent behind our ACAV that was a rally point for any wounded soldiers. As the battle increased in intensity we started to receive a number of wounded men into the tent. One was Sergeant Raines who had a bullet wound to the chest. Our medic was overwhelmed with multiple patients and shouted to me to take a look at Rob. I opened the front of his shirt and saw a small hole that was slowly pumping blood out. I applied a large compression bandage to his chest and pushed down to stop the bleeding. I started to talk to him, but he wasn't responding, so I called to Doc that I needed him now. Doc took a look at Rob's chest wound and quickly turned him over to expose an exit wound that had taken a large part of his back out. Rob died within minutes with Doc telling me there was nothing we could have done to save him.

In writing this story I went online to research Rob's name and found an article where his home town of Greenwood, Indiana recognized him in 2015. A member of the local Greenwood VFW Post 5864 constructed a handmade flag display case and presented it to Rob's brother Rick. I found Rick's email and sent him a short note identifying myself and letting him know Rob's memory is still alive. I was a little apprehensive about sending the note, not knowing if it would open sad memories from long ago. I received a letter back from Rick, who served in Vietnam with the 25th Infantry Division for a year before Rob and I was relieved that he was so gracious that Rob's memory is still alive. To Rick and Rob's family, may God bless and for Rob to rest in peace.

Though the horrors of war will always be etched in the back of my mind, the images are somewhat outweighed by the comradery I had with my fellow soldiers. We were in a position that most people will never imagine and we relied on men we had only known for a short time to have our backs. War provides a certain bond that lasts a lifetime even if the names and faces fade into the ages.

One name and face that will never fade is Bill Smith. Bill was a Southern California guy and we hit it off immediately when I joined the 11th Cav. We kept in touch after we were discharged and in the spring of 1971 he called me and said, "How would you like to come out west and spend the summer in Arizona"? He indicated we would have jobs working as bouncers at a night club on the Colorado River called Rum Runners Retreat. I was in college and had the summer free so how could I pass that up? So one morning in June a friend of mine, Mike Howard, dropped me off at the entrance to the Mass Pike at Copley Square and I began hitchhiking to Arizona. Yes, hitchhiking. Five days later after numerous rides I met Bill at Rum Runners and we had a great summer working at the bar from Friday through Monday and enjoying Arizona and Southern California the rest of the week. Rum Runners was right on the Colorado River and boats could hook up to its dock. It was packed all weekend and we worked long hours. We weren't paid much, but we did get to eat and drink for free which more than made up for the low pay. Most of our time was spent flirting with girls rather than breaking up fights. Though there was one time that caused me some concern. It was a busy afternoon and Bill came up to me and said some guy was causing problems and we had to throw him out. We went over to a pool table where he was playing and I was looking at the biggest person I ever saw. He was over 6'5" and must have weighed at least 300 pounds. And he was all muscle. Bill went over to him and said, "Hey a#@%, you're outta here." The next thing that happened stunned me. Instead of this behemoth pounding us into submission he hugged Bill and said, "How have you been?" The giant pool player was Ron Yary, the number one pick in the 1968 NFL draft and a former teammate of Bill's at USC. Needless to say I had a sigh of relief. When the summer ended I hitchhiked back to Boston just in time for school to start. Bill and I have kept in touch over the years via letters and phone calls and I had the opportunity to visit with him and his wife Barb one time when I was in San Francisco on business.

A good part of my hitchhiking adventure took me down the old Route 66. On my 5th day on the road I find myself standing on a corner in Winslow, Arizona with my thumb out for a ride. All of a sudden it's a girl, my Lord, not in a flatbed Ford, but a VW Beatle slowing down to take a look at me. A minute later after circling the block she pulls up and asks me if I want a ride. I ask her where she is going and it is totally the opposite direction from where I am headed. So we may lose and we may win and I knew I'd never be there again, but I didn't climb in. This was June of 1971 and the Eagles came out with "Take it Easy" in May 1972. So thank you song writers Glen Frey and Jackson Browne

When the 11th Cav returned home from Vietnam they were eventually sent to Germany where they pulled duty for many years and

M-48 Patton Tank

continued their image of excellence. The unit was so good they were eventually transferred to Fort Irwin, California, where they are now the national training brigade for the Army preparing other combat units for deployment to the Middle East. They have mockups of Middle Eastern villages and run soldiers through various live fire exercises to give them a realistic vision of what they can expect when they get to the real thing.

So to Black Horse soldiers past and present, keep "Finding the Bastards and Piling On."

M-155 self-propelled Howitzer

50-caliber machine gun

ACAV's ready to rumble

M-551 Sheridan Tank

A Chu Hoi – North
Vietnamese Army
defector who became
our translator

John with Al Curry
(Chicago)

Beautiful day in the
neighborhood

Bill Smith

Bill Smith: It's not Laguna Beach

Captured Viet Cong rocket propelled
grenade launcher

M-60 Machine Gun Belts

Circle the wagons

Hole in sign from an RPG

RPG damage to an ACAV

CHAIN LINK FENCE

I am looking through a hole in a chain link fence and see soldiers running from tank to tank, flares popping off in mid-air and mortar shells landing around our perimeter. The sight, sound, and smells are familiar, but then I realize, I should not be seeing this.

Why in a conflict where billions of dollars are being spent on weaponry, vehicles, aircraft, and ammunition is a simple inexpensive 10-foot roll of chain link fence one of our most valuable assets?

When we are in a 12-ton armored cavalry assault vehicle (ACAV) we have tremendous fire power, but we also command a significant amount of attention from the enemy. As we rumble through the jungle they can hear us coming from miles away. When we set up in a night defensive position no camouflage is going to hide that giant metal container that is our home. So even with this superior fire power we are still vulnerable.

The enemy weapon that is of most concern to us is the Rocket Propelled Grenade (RPG). The easiest description would be to call it a baby bazooka. Looking like a toy, but carrying quite a wallop, it is a three-foot long tube that is shoulder-fired with a war head that is about a foot long. If an RPG round lands in the middle of troops in the open it will ruin their whole day with its shell fragments and shrapnel. But for those of us in armored vehicles it poses a more deadly threat.

The war head is a High Explosive Anti-Tank (HEAT) round. If the round hits the armored wall of our vehicle the force of energy heats the metal to an incredibly high temperature that creates an opening for the explosive. The explosive literally eats through the 3-inch-thick armored plating and exits with a hole larger than where it entered. Anything or anybody inside or on top of the vehicle is peppered with the rounds of shell fragments as well as the metal coming off the vehicle. Needless to say it is not a position we want to be in.

We developed a simple way to protect ourselves from the HEAT round's intensity. When we set up our night defensive position, we place one inexpensive 10 foot length of chain link fence in front of our vehicle and another one covering the rear. If an RPG hits the chain link it explodes immediately and even though it is still dangerous the high impact energy destruction from hitting the tank directly is dissipated.

So one day our unit sets up our night defensive position as usual. Because we arrived at the site earlier than expected we take the opportunity to fill about 100 sandbags for added protection. We stack the sandbags about four feet high and ten feet long across the rear area of our vehicle. We then stake in the chain link fence in front of the sandbags. After deciding on the guard duty rotation for our vehicle I set up my bed roll behind the sand-bagged wall to get some much needed sleep.

Sometime in the middle of the night I am awakened by the sounds of battle. It takes a few seconds for me to register what is happening. That is when I see soldiers running from tank to tank, flares popping off in mid-air, mortar rounds landing around our perimeter. Then I remember I should not be seeing any of this, there should be a wall of sandbags in front of me. I am fully awake now and I see that there is a hole in the chain link fence and I am covered in dirt from the sand-bagged wall that is knocked over. Luckily the RPG that was destined for our vehicle initially hit the chain link fence, detonated the round, and then the force of the explosion was absorbed by the sandbags.

Needless to say, this simple inexpensive protection was more important that night than any of the elaborate weapons we had in our arsenal. And if I didn't have that chain link fence, I would probably not be writing this story.

Note the chain link fence

An M-551 that didn't make it

I REMEMBER WILLIE

I just got off the phone after talking with Ricky Johnson for an hour and a half about his dad, Willie. Willie was a 35-year-old African American from South Carolina, with a wife and six kids. What did I, a 20-year-old single white kid from Quincy, Massachusetts have in common with him, other than being stationed in Vietnam with the 11th Armored Cavalry Regiment? Well, living with someone in an Armored Cavalry Assault Vehicle (ACAV) for five months will make for close relationships.

Willie was a career military soldier, our first sergeant, a leader, advisor, confessor, and friend. He was firm but fair and full of life. He even taught me to play pinochle, a card game I had never played before meeting him and have never played since. Also, I never called him Willie, it was always "Top." Top is a standard term of affection for a First Sergeant. He was killed by a rocket propelled grenade (RPG) just a few feet from me. One thing about combat is that there is no rhyme or reason why some men survive and others don't.

March 5, 1970 was much like any other day in Vietnam as we moved from a location near the Cambodian border to another just four or five miles away. The rolling hill terrain with thick forest was always a challenge for our 12-ton armored vehicles. It didn't help that the temperature was constantly in the 90s with similar humidity and mosquitos swarming around our heads. We arrived at our night defensive position a little before dusk and deployed our 20 ACAVs similar to the way covered wagons would circle up in western movies. The track commander was Captain Max Bailey who sat on the top of our vehicle behind a 50- caliber machine gun, the driver was Don whose last name I forget, and Top and I were the rear gunners behind M-60 machine guns. I dismounted our track, set up trip flares covering our part of the perimeter, and positioned claymore mines in front of our vehicle. We had been in constant contact with the enemy for the previous three or four months and were always prepared for battle. I cleaned my weapons, an M-16 automatic rifle and the M-60 machine gun, daily. We knew our job and were always ready for action. Our enemy was not the Viet Cong but the North Vietnamese Army (NVA), a highly trained and well-equipped fighting group and we never knew where or when they would hit us.

I was still awake, probably around 10:00 pm, when I heard the distinctive thump of a mortar tube being fired. Seconds later the first rounds hit in and around our perimeter. This is when I can use the old cliché "that all hell broke loose." The mortar rounds were followed immediately by a barrage of enemy AK-47 and RPG fire, and we responded in kind with our own volleys of machine gun and tank cannon fire. With 20 vehicles firing at once the sound was deafening and the smell of cordite filled the air. We knew we were in for a tough battle as even with our superior fire power the enemy kept up their attack. Ground and aerial flares lit the night sky and claymore mines exploded all around the perimeter as the enemy closed in.

As in most combat situations the actual battle seems longer than it really is. With our superior weapons and withering fire power the enemy attack finally died down after about 20 or 30 minutes. But this is when we worry the most. We have been on an adrenaline high during the battle and now we come back down to earth and reassess. Captain Bailey dismounted our vehicle and walked the perimeter to check on damage and the wounded. Willie, Don and I pulled up more ammunition for our weapons and waited for the next anticipated attack. A while later Top received a call from Captain Bailey that some wounded enemy had been spotted in a bomb crater a few ACAVs down from us.

We had a directive from our headquarters' G-2 Intelligence that if we had the opportunity we should try to take prisoners for interrogation. Top was one of those soldiers who would never order someone to do something that he wouldn't do himself. So he jumped off our vehicle and told Don and me to follow him down our perimeter to get more information. When we got to where the enemy was sighted Captain Bailey confirmed that he was pretty sure there were two or three wounded NVA about 30-40 meters from our perimeter. Without blinking, Top said, "Let's go get them." So Top, Don, Captain Bailey, and I lined up about five meters apart and headed for the bomb crater.

Because I respected Top as a soldier I had no problem following his lead. We made it about halfway to the crater when a figure jumped up with an RPG and fired at us. The rocket landed between Top and Don who were at the end of our line. With that "all hell broke loose" again. We received more incoming mortar and RPG rounds that were soon followed by enemy small arms fire. I hit the dirt and returned fire at the shadowy figure. Unfortunately I was now caught about 20 meters outside of our perimeter. I lost sight of the other three as bullets whistled above me. Just as concerned about the friendly fire from behind as the enemy fire in front, I gathered my wits and slowly crawled back to our perimeter. Back inside the perimeter I looked for Top, Don and Captain Bailey, but couldn't find them. As the battle raged on I returned to my ACAV, took up my position and continued to return fire. When the other three hadn't returned I just assumed they jumped on other ACAVs to continue the battle. Eventually things quieted down and this time we were sure the enemy had retreated. Sometime later Captain Bailey returned to our vehicle and that is when he told me that Willie was killed by the RPG round and Don was wounded. Captain Bailey was also wounded, but he continued to lead the battle and was awarded the Silver Star for his efforts. I was stunned. I had been in country for 10 months and through a lot. Although other men in my unit had paid the ultimate sacrifice this was different. Because I was so close to Top it hit me hard. It was made worse because I had to stay alert and man my vehicle in case there was another attack. I had to wait until morning and there was nothing I could do except live with whatever thoughts were going through my head. It was no consolation that later on I found out the two enemy soldiers were killed.

You don't plan for someone to get killed so you don't know how to react. At first light I went over to the medical area and saw Top's body on the ground covered with a rubber poncho. I can't remember if I cried, but I was in a state of disbelief. Here was a person I truly respected, who I confided in, told stories with, and a few short hours before had been laughing and joking with, and now he was gone.

I am at my computer about 33 years later, Vietnam a memory long in the past, but with me every day. Vietnam not only defined a generation, it also defines us personally. It is hard not to think often about something that unique. I am on the 11th Armored Cavalry website that provides a wealth of information about our time in country. One of the data points is a list of the 700 11th Cav Troopers who were killed in Vietnam. I go to the list and scroll to Top's name. Over the years I have thought about him many times and often wonder how the family he left behind fared. The website includes a message board that anyone can access. I scroll down past some of the messages and freeze when I see one signed by a Ricky Johnson who wants to hear from anyone who had served with his dad Willie who died on March 5, 1970.

After a few deep breaths and a couple of stiff drinks I summon the courage to give Ricky a call. It is extremely emotional and I have all I can do to keep it together. Ricky was 11 years old when Willie was killed leaving his wife Lillie to raise Ricky and his five siblings. It is heartwarming to learn that all six children have graduated from college, married, and have families of their own. Ricky has two children close in ages to mine and his mother is doing well still living in South Carolina. A disconcerting part of the call is learning that the Army never told the family how Willie had died. It is very difficult as I recount the events of that night, but it is a step closer to the closure that neither of us will probably ever achieve.

For a year in Vietnam we are thrown into a situation where our lives depend on the actions of men we have just recently met. We become as close to them as we would a brother. We are with them 24/7 eating, talking, laughing and trying to stay alive. Then our tour of duty is over, we return to our hometown and begin a new life. As time goes by, memories start to fade about certain events, and even the names of the comrades we were so close to are forgotten. But for the rest of my life I will remember Willie and all that he taught me, but mostly I will remember him as a friend.

To all the Willie Johnsons who never came home, may you always be remembered.

Willie "Top" Johnson

WHO WANTS TO BE A MILLIONAIRE?

Well maybe not a millionaire, but there was an opportunity that I could have cashed in big time, even in Vietnam.

My last three days stateside before going overseas were spent at Fort Lewis Washington. It was pretty relaxing with nothing to do but wait for my flight to be scheduled to go to Vietnam. I could sleep as much as I wanted, have the run of the base activity centers, and spend time at the enlisted men's club. This was all in anticipation of what was ultimately in store for me. Finally my plane was scheduled and off I went for an 18-hour flight to Vietnam with a few hours layover in Tokyo.

What was the first thing I did when processing in country? If you guessed being issued a weapon you'd be wrong. The first thing was setting up a bank account. Even in war capitalism rules. My paycheck would be automatically deposited into the US bank on the base and the balance would earn 10% interest. Both the automatic deposit and the rate of interest were unheard of stateside. It was explained that there wasn't much I'd be able to spend my money on, given where I was going, so I might as well put it all in the bank. Of course, being a GI, I knew that I could probably find something to spend my money on no matter where I was. So I had about $50 a month given to me in cash and the rest put in the bank. My deposit wasn't that much as my salary as a private first class with combat and hazardous duty pay was only $192 a month. After five months, a promotion to Spec 4 and then to sergeant swelled my pay to $350 a month.

The next step was to replace all of my green backs (American dollars) with Military Payment Certificates (MPC). MPCs were the same denominations as green backs, $1, $5, $10 and $20, but were different colors and had different designs. Instead of dead presidents the designs were of military equipment like tanks, battleships and B-52s. I next got the lecture about financial transactions with the local Vietnamese people. It was strictly prohibited to use MPC for any local purchases. If I wanted to buy from a local I had to go to a bank on the airbase and exchange the MPC for Vietnamese piasters, the local currency. The going rate was 118 piasters for $1 in MPC. It was also explained that the reason for this was to keep the MPC from flowing into the black market and upsetting the Vietnamese economy. This was all well and good, except that I and most other GIs in country were never at the airbase to legally exchange our MPC. What realistically happened was we would exchange with the local villagers and get a better exchange rate of 150 piasters to the $1 MPC.

No matter where I was deployed there were usually small villages nearby. So I actually did get a chance to spend money on some trinkets or a cold beer or two. Of course, against the rules, I would exchange the MPC for piasters with the locals.

Then one day with no warning a chopper swooped into our area and we were told to line up in front of a table that was set up on the landing zone. A couple of officers exited the chopper with two large metal containers. One container was empty and the other was full of brand new MPC, but with different colors and designs. The black market in illegally-exchanged MPC had definitely played havoc with the Vietnamese economy and as a result, the powers that be decided that in order to stabilize the economy they needed to remove all of the old MPC from circulation. So they decided to swap all old MPC with new ones throughout the country in one day. It was made perfectly clear that once the chopper left the ground no further MPC would be exchanged. The swapping was only done with the GIs in country and rendered the MPC held by the Vietnamese worthless. So we just threw our old MPC into one container and were issued an equal value in new ones from the other container.

Whatever havoc the black-market exchange of MPC caused in the Vietnamese economy, it paled to the havoc in the local village the next morning. Once the villagers learned that the old MPC was worthless, they descended on us from all directions. Old men, old women, young boys and girls all with fistfuls of old MPC were crying and begging us to swap their old ones for our new ones at a great discount. One older Vietnamese who I recognized as a village leader came up to me with a bag of B-52s, $20 bills. The currency was neatly wrapped, 100 bills in a stack and there were five stacks, $10,000 in all. All he wanted was $50 in new MPC as a trade. My first inclination was "why not", as there could be a way to convince some high-level officer that somehow I was overlooked when the chopper came to exchange our money. Then I realized I was pretty sure I would be questioned as to what I was doing with $10,000 when I was making $350 a month. So not wanting to spend the rest of my tour in LBJ (Long Binh Jail), I politely declined.

So it wasn't a million, but it was quite a lot. But it was never realistic. It was years before I ever made $10,000 in one year let alone one day.

AUTOMATIC AMBUSH

The claymore mine is one of the nastier weapons in our armament toolbox. It is about ten inches long, four inches high, and two inches wide. That doesn't sound like much, but add a backing of one pound of C-4 plastic explosive and 400 ¼ inch steel ball bearings and you can imagine what damage it can cause. The claymore is usually deployed in front of our position pointed in the direction we think an attack will be coming. A dynamite cap is inserted into the C-4 in the claymore and a 50-foot wire is run back to our defensive position where it is attached to an electronic hand-held plunger. When we engage the plunger an electronic signal detonates the dynamite cap, which explodes the C-4, which sends the 400 ball bearings in a 60-degree angle towards the enemy. Anyone who is within 25-50 meters of this salvo has their entire day ruined. The design of the claymore results in minimum blowback and to err on the side of safety there is an inscription on the device that reads "this side toward enemy."

Beginning with the American Revolution, through the Civil War, World War I, World War II, and Korea the American soldier's battle plan was simply to start at Point A, engage the enemy, capture territory and continue to move the line until the battle or war was won. Vietnam changed all that. It was the first time American forces fought a guerilla war with no territorial objective. We took an area one day, moved on, and the enemy infiltrated the area again the next day. In addition, in many cases we were blind to the enemy. The kindly farmer in the local village by day was actually a Viet Cong soldier by night. Roads that were safe by day had 40-pound mines imbedded in them at night. Trip wires connected to a hand grenade were placed on trails commonly travelled by American soldiers. It took the strategists a while to figure this out and adjust the game plan.

As a member of both the 82nd Airborne Division and then the 11th Armored Cavalry Regiment our main strategy was to set up nighttime ambush patrols where we could beat the enemy at their own game. Whether it was a 10-man infantry squad or a group of Armored Cavalry

Assault Vehicles the procedure was the same. We scouted out an area where there was possible enemy movement, then waited until nightfall to set up our position. Sometimes we reset our position to confuse the enemy if we thought they were observing. We then set up our night defensive position with trip flares and claymore mines and waited for the enemy to approach. Of course, there were many nights when there was no action as the enemy realized we were in the area. Thus was born the "automatic ambush."

The automatic ambush was the brainchild of someone in the 11th Cav. Based on the best intelligence we determined potential places the enemy would travel at night and discreetly visited the area late in the day to set up our automatic ambush. We placed five or six claymore mines about 10 feet apart alongside a trail we thought the enemy would be using. Angling the claymores to cover a large part of the trail from front to back we armed each device with a dynamite cap and ran the sets of detonating wire back to the beginning of the trail. About six inches above the end of each detonating wire we stripped off a two- or three-inch length of rubber exposing the copper wire and twisted them together to form one solid piece of exposed wire. We staked a large nine-volt battery into the ground and placed the bottom of the rubber-coated wire across the positive and negative poles, being careful not to have the exposed copper wire come in contact with the poles. We attached a trip wire to a tree across the front of the trail and wrapped it around the unexposed end of the detonating wire. We then moved to a position two or three miles away. When the first enemy soldier hit the trip wire it pulled the exposed detonating wire across the positive and negative poles and simultaneously set off all of the claymores. If you can imagine the damage of one claymore, imagine the power of five or six. In the dead of night the explosion of five or six claymores sounded like it was right next to us. In addition, we provided the exact coordinates to our mortar crews who then laid in 10 or 15 high explosive rounds for good measure. We waited until daylight to move in and assess the damage.

We used this technique dozens of times. Sometimes we went the entire night and had no explosions. The next morning when we arrived at the site we were very careful in disarming the devices. Sometimes after an explosion we arrived and just saw great damage to the trees and vegetation, probably set off by a small animal. And then there were other times when it was not a pleasant sight.

From captured soldiers we got word that these automatic ambushes were having a profound effect on the enemy's psyche. They were more afraid of our new tactics than of our traditional bombing and artillery fire.

It took us a while, but we did beat the enemy at their own game.

THE TALE OF BOBBY PHILLIPS

It's a Saturday afternoon early in July 1970. I'm sitting in Dee Dee's Lounge and Grill in the Wollaston neighborhood of Quincy, Massachusetts. Dee Dee's is the consummate neighborhood bar that has that ingrained smell of stale beer, cheap drinks, and good pizza; is full of eclectic customers with interesting nicknames (Masher, Hugga, Boydo, Dago, Woji, Oakie, Fuzzy, Campy, Rock); has lots of sports photos on the wall and is a great place to meet your buddies to decide what is in store for the rest of the day. While I am waiting I see a copy of yesterday's Quincy Patriot Ledger, the daily newspaper specifically covering Quincy but with state and national news as well. I glimpse the front page and below the fold I see the headline, "Former Quincy Man Missing in Action (MIA) in Vietnam." The story goes on to indicate that a Robert Phillips, formerly of the Montclair section of North Quincy, was reported missing in action. I was stunned for two reasons. One, I had just returned from my one-year tour of duty in Vietnam and having lost a number of friends to the war, any loss hit home, especially if it was someone from Quincy. And two, I had just been with Bobby three months earlier!

On April 10, 1970, I was sitting on the tarmac of Bien Hoa Airbase just outside of Saigon. My tour of duty was over and I was one of the lucky ones to be going home in one piece. I waited patiently to hop on a Freedom Bird for the trip back to the world when all of a sudden I saw this soldier walking past me and I instantly recognized Bobby Phillips. Bobby was one of my best friends in junior high school and my first year of high school. He was a great kid, fun to be with, full of mischief, and always getting into trouble. Maybe that was why we hit it off so well. Bobby's family moved away from Quincy after his freshman year and like many relationships during that era we lost touch. There was no Facebook or Instagram or cell phones to keep people connected no matter where they are. Bobby had moved to Ohio and he was just finishing up his second tour of duty in Vietnam. He was slated to return home sometime in August and was planning to move back to Quincy.

We caught up as best we could in the short time we had and vowed to reconnect once he returned to Quincy.

I'm back at Dee Dee's re-reading the short account in the Patriot Ledger and wondering how this could have happened. Bobby had been in Vietnam for almost two years, but he told me he had a great assignment. He was a truck driver and his day usually consisted of driving from Bien Hoa to downtown Saigon to pick up civilian workers who did a lot of the manual labor around the airbase. He would then drive the workers back to Saigon later in the afternoon. In between he would transport supplies from Bien Hoa to smaller fire bases that rimmed the city. All in all it was a boring, but safe job. I was at a loss to find out any more of what had happened. He had no family in the area and I had no idea where his family was in Ohio. I continued to read the newspapers for any follow up story that had more details. But there was nothing. In 1973 when the US left Vietnam and all of the prisoners of war (POWs) came home I thought I would find Bobby's name among them, but I didn't. Months turned into years and like so many other veterans I got on with my life. I went to college, started a career, got married, and raised a family. All the time in the back of my mind I wondered what had happened to Bobby.

It is now the mid 1990's and the internet had opened up research to levels never before seen. I search for Bobby's name and military experience, and find an official Army "After Action Report" that pieces together what had happened to him.

As it turns out Bobby was not MIA, but was a POW. The After Action Report indicated that Bobby and two other soldiers had an assignment to deliver supplies to a fire base further away from Saigon than the normal route. They could reach the destination two ways. Even though they were told that one road was thought to be mined, the sergeant in charge decided to take that route anyway. So early in the afternoon Bobby, the sergeant and another soldier set out on their journey. About three hours later their truck was ambushed and the three men went missing. Many of the details in the After Action Report were provided by captured Viet Cong soldiers and the North Vietnam government. A captured enemy soldier indicated that he was part of the ambush and one of the GIs, identified as the sergeant, was killed and the other two were taken prisoner. From the accounts, for the next 18 months Bobby was moved dozens of times throughout South Vietnam and Cambodia from one prisoner camp to another. Early in his capture he tried to escape, but the attempt failed. Then one night after almost a year and a half in captivity wearing only the clothes he had on when he was captured, Bobby tried to escape again. This time he was successful and for a short time he survived in the surrounding jungles. I can't imagine how frightening it was for him, constantly moving, foraging for food, evading his captors, with nothing but the clothes on his back. Unfortunately, he was soon re-captured, brought back to his prison camp and because of his actions, was executed. His body was never recovered and to this day there is still no closure for his family and friends.

Staff Sergeant Robert Phillips's name may be etched in black marble on Panel 9W of the Vietnam Memorial, but Bobby Phillip's memory will forever be etched in my mind.

TRIBUTE TO NORTH QUINCY HIGH SCHOOL

My current home is Plymouth, Massachusetts and I have previously lived in Duxbury, MA for 27 years and Waltham MA for 10 years. My true hometown is Quincy, more specifically North Quincy, where I am a proud graduate of **North Quincy High School Class of 1967.** I still attend as many football and basketball games as I can, and have had the honor to speak to the student body on a few occasions. My time at North Quincy gave me many memories and, more importantly, many good friends who I still keep in touch with to this day. A group of us get together for lunch at the local 99 Restaurant every three or four weeks. I really look forward to seeing Ross Ajemian, Kenny McPhee, Ricky Williamson, Rick Nash, Freddy Cobban, Stevie Martinson, Jerry Mulvey, Danny Marini, Mike Howard, George Duguay, Eddie Miller, and Jimmy Ducey to have lively discussions about sports and politics and relive tales of our teenage adventures.

North Quincy High School is a beautiful building; I guess you would call it Greek revival architecture. Opened in 1933 it has lots of character with columns and distinctive carvings. No modern steel and glass for this structure. When you enter the main lobby you pass an impressive display case with many trophies, plaques and mementos of various sports achievements of the past. But more impressive is when you walk into a three-story tiered atrium that is referred to as the Hall of Heroes.

On the walls are plaques with the names of North Quincy graduates who gave their lives in defense of our country. There are 25 names from World War II, three from the Korean War, one from the War on Terror, and 12 from my generation, Vietnam, that I will talk about later. There are also five large banners hanging from the ceiling that honor five special North Quincy graduates who went above and beyond their calls of duty.

The first banner honors Captain Everett Pope, Company C, 1st Marine Division, **NQHS Class of 1936**. On the night of September 19, 1944 in the Battle of Peleliu Island Captain Pope led his men in the defense of a strategic hill. Despite being largely outnumbered and outgunned, Captain Pope deployed his men smartly and repeatedly drove back the Japanese attackers. In the morning with little ammunition left, Captain Pope resorted to using empty ammunition cans, rocks and finally hand to hand combat to ward off the enemy and lead the remainder of his company to safety. For his leadership and bravery, Captain Pope was awarded the Congressional Medal of Honor.

The next banner honors Private First Class (PFC) William Cady, 3rd Battalion, 5th Marine Division, **NQHS Class of 1942**. At the Battle of Iwo Jima on March 3rd, 1945 moving forward to attack a Japanese machine gun nest, an enemy hand grenade was thrown in the midst of his squad. Without hesitation PFC William Cady threw himself on the grenade and paid the ultimate sacrifice to save his squad members. For this action PFC William Cady was awarded the Congressional Medal of Honor.

North Quincy High School is one of only three schools in America that can boast of having multiple Medal of Honor recipients. The other two are Pueblo Central High School in Pueblo, Colorado and New Hanover High School in Wilmington, North Carolina.

The third banner honors someone from a different generation. Captain Richard Stratton, US Navy, **NQHS Class of 1958**. A naval aviator shot down over North Vietnam on January 5, 1967, Captain Stratton spent just over six years at the Hanoi Hilton under constant physical and mental torture. As we go through our everyday lives with problems like traffic jams and cloudy days at the beach, think about what Captain Stratton had to endure.

The fourth banner honors Captain Alan Brudno, US Air Force **NQHS Class of 1960.** An Air Force fighter pilot, Captain Brudno was shot down over North Vietnam on October 18, 1965. Alan had the dubious distinction of being held in captivity 2,675 days, almost seven and a half years, the 2nd longest time of any POW in Vietnam. Again, like Captain Stratton, it is impossible to imagine what those seven and a half years were like. I will elaborate on Captain Brudno's legacy later in this story.

The final banner honors Major Charles Sweeny, US Army Air Corp,

NQHS Class of 1937. Many people have no idea who Major Sweeny was, but it can be argued that he brought World War II to an end. Wow, that is quite a statement.

Charles Sweeny was a self-taught pilot, and a good one at that. He learned to fly at Dennison Airport in the Squantum section of North Quincy that is now the luxury Marina Bay Complex. Charles enlisted in the Army Air Corp, which was the forerunner of the US Air Force, soon after graduating from North Quincy High School. When World War II broke out he envisioned himself flying combat missions over Europe or the Pacific. But that wasn't to be. Charles was such a good pilot that the military leaders thought he could better serve his country by training other pilots. And that is what he did for the next three years. He trained hundreds if not thousands of men to become pilots. These pilots went on to dominate the skies and assure the Allied powers of air superiority that eventually led to victory.

Though he spent most of his time during World War II stateside, he did see his dream fulfilled as he actually was able to fly two combat missions near the end of the war. His second and last combat mission was on August 9, 1945. You see, Major Charles Sweeny, **NQHS Class of 1937,** flew the plane that dropped the atomic bomb on Nagasaki, bringing Japan to its knees and forcing its surrender.

As I mentioned, this was his second combat mission. His first mission was three days earlier where he flew as the wingman for Colonel Paul Tibbets and the Enola Gay that dropped the first atomic bomb on Hiroshima. Ironically, Colonel Tibbets was born in Quincy, Illinois.

So these are five special NQHS graduates who will go down in the annals of history. I also want to introduce you to 12 other NQHS grads, who may not meet the standards of the above five, but are heroes in their own right. I knew most of them as they were either friends, teammates or neighbors.

Ricky Vasconcellos, Private First Class, USMC, **NQHS Class of 1965.** His family owned a small grocery store right up the street from the high school on the corner of Hunt Street and Newbury Ave. Ironically, the store has been owned for many years by a Vietnamese family. We always stopped at the store on the way home from football or basketball practice to have a soda or ice cream and talk with Ricky's sister, Marina. Ricky left school early to enlist in the Marine Corp and was sent to Vietnam in the spring of 1966. During a routine patrol on August 15th a hidden M-26 hand grenade placed as a booby trap was tripped and the explosion wounded two other Marines and killed Ricky. As Ricky was the first from North Quincy to give his life it had a profound impact on all of us. Though the network news reported nightly on the war, Ricky's death brought it all home. He was 19 years old and is buried at Arlington National Cemetery.

Ralph Willard, Warrant Officer, 1st Air Cavalry Division, US Army, **NQHS Class of 1965.** Ralph enlisted in the Army as a private, but was accepted into the Army's aviation school where he became a helicopter pilot. On the night of July 21, 1968 Ralph flew a dangerous re-supply mission to an infantry outpost under siege. As he attempted to land, his helicopter took massive enemy fire and crashed killing all aboard. Ralph had only been in country for three months and was 20 years old. He was awarded the Distinguished Flying Cross.

Beaver Ahern, Lance Corporal, USMC, **NQHS Class of 1965.** Though his name was Brian we all called him Beaver as in "Leave it to Beaver." He came from a family of Marines as his older brother Mark and two younger brothers Taylor and Dana were also Jarheads. One of the most powerful monuments in Washington, DC is the Vietnam Veterans Memorial Wall. Because I worked for the Federal government and traveled to Washington often, I visited the Memorial many times. The simple black marble slab with over 58,000 names etched into its surface is visited by more people than any other memorial in DC. It is hard to explain the effect the wall has as you start at one end that is only a foot high and move slowly to the apex in the middle that is over 10 feet high. As you proceed down the wall with the many other visitors it becomes eerily quiet as you realize every inch of the slab is covered with the names of fathers, sons and brothers and yes, eight daughters. The highly polished marble catches your reflection and for that moment you become part of the memorial. Beaver was killed on January 7, 1968. His name can be found on Panel 33E-Line 63. He was 20 years old.

George Fell, Specialist Four, 25th Infantry Division, US Army, **NQHS Class of 1965.** Boy, did the girls love George. We always wanted to be with George as the girls would flock to him. It wasn't just because he was good looking. He was sensitive and sincere and really knew how to talk to the opposite sex, while the rest of us just fumbled around. George had only two months left in his tour when on May 23, 1970 he was killed by a rocket explosion during the invasion of Cambodia. George was 22 years old. This was especially hard for me, as I had gotten home just a month earlier and here I was going to his funeral.

David Sullivan, Lance Corporal, USMC, **NQHS Class of 1967.** Dave also left school early to join the Marine Corps. On the night of February 14, 1969 David was point man for his platoon during an assault on enemy positions near the Ashua Valley. He detected four NVA soldiers manning a machine gun and threw a hand grenade killing two of the enemy. Disregarding his own safety, David pursued the other two enemy killing both. On his way back to rejoin his platoon he was mortally wounded by an enemy sniper. For his heroic actions he was awarded the Silver Star. David was 20 years old.

Marty Keefe, Lance Corporal, USMC, **NQHS Class of 1967.** Marty was a big happy-go-lucky kid who was a teammate on our undefeated championship football team. He enlisted in the Marines right after high school and went to Vietnam in April of 1968. On February 23, 1969 the 3rd Force recon platoon set up an ambush along the Cua Viet River in Quang Tri Province. Around 3:15 in the morning the team observed 20 Viet Cong soldiers moving toward the river. As part of the Marine's support they had US Navy PBRs (river patrol boats) at the ready. After the initial engagement some of the enemy closed within 15 yards of the Marines' position. The ambush patrol requested support from the PBRs which responded with M-79 grenade launcher and 50-caliber machine gun fire. Marty was hit with a 50-caliber round of friendly fire and died immediately. He was 20 years old.

Larry Sirios, Corporal, USMC, **NQHS Class of 1967.** Why did we call him Bucket? I am sure we had a reason, but it has been so long ago,

I can't remember why. On November 24, 1968 Company H made contact with a large North Vietnamese Army (NVA) force in a heavily fortified area. As Company H assaulted the NVA bunkers they were met with withering fire. Though the enemy was routed, the Marines suffered six losses. Larry was one of them. I came home on leave about a month after Larry was killed. My mom who was a good friend of Mrs. Sirios told me they were on the phone together when Mrs. Sirios said, "Jennie, I have to hang up. There is a Marine officer with a priest walking down the driveway." She knew it wasn't good news. Larry was 20 years old.

Peter Gerry, Specialist Four, A Company, 2nd Battalion, 25th Infantry Division, **NQHS Class of 1968.** Peter enlisted in the Army right out of high school and became a combat medic. He was in country only three months when he was killed by small arms fire on July 28, 1969. A remembrance from his brother Billy written in 2015 underscores the effect losing someone to war has on a family. "It's been 46 years and I still think, love and pray every day to you. Now Mom, Dad, Stephen and Michael have joined you. I can only wonder what their faces looked like when they met up with you. Someday, I will see your smiling face along with everybody else. Today I am in Washington DC, will be visiting the wall for the sixth time. It's never easy, but nothing close to what you endured during your final few months in Vietnam. Love you more than you can understand." Peter was 18 years old.

Chris Donahue, Lance Corporal, C Battery, 1st Battalion, 1st Division, USMC, **NQHS Class of 1968.** Chris was still in high school when he enlisted and went to Vietnam five months after he graduated. He was killed on May 19, 1969. Chris was 18 years old.

Gary Webb, Private First Class, C Company, 1st Battalion, USMC, **NQHS Class of 1968.** Gary went to Vietnam on June 6, 1969 and was killed on June 22, 1969, just 16 days into his tour. Gary was 18 years old.

James Stark, Sergeant US Air Force, **NQHS Class of 1964.** Jimmy grew up just a few streets from me. He was a few years older than me and I can remember him as a really tough kid that we didn't want to mess around with. He had less than two months left in his tour when he died on January 24, 1968. Jimmy was 21 years old.

Alan Brudno, Captain, US Navy, **NQHS Class of 1960.** As I mentioned in the beginning of this story Captain Brudno was a POW for seven and a half years. His is one of the saddest stories of the Vietnam War. Alan came home with the other 565 POWs in 1973. But, like most Vietnam War veterans, he didn't come home to a welcoming country. There were no parades or brass bands and no banners hanging from the overpasses on Route 3. Alan just came home and four months later he took his own life. At the time no one really understood the hidden consequences of depression that combat soldiers go through. Especially the severe aspects endured by POWs. Post-Traumatic Stress Disorder (PTSD) would not be officially diagnosed until 1980. However, Alan's death was not in vain as it was a wakeup call to the armed forces that they needed to address psychological issues in a formal manner and not just let individuals figure things out on their own. Unfortunately, it has taken a long time to bring this issue to the forefront and to have it properly addressed. Alan took his life the day before his 33rd birthday.

I'm a Raider, I'm a Raider, I'm a Raider 'til I die!
(NQHS Fight Song)

Postscript: In 1987 the City of Quincy dedicated an 80-foot clock tower at the Marina Bay Complex to commemorate the 48 men from Quincy who gave their lives in Vietnam. Besides the 12 who graduated from North Quincy High School, there were 19 who graduated from Quincy High School, one who graduated from Archbishop Williams High School, and 16 who either grew up in Quincy but moved away before they entered the service, or moved to Quincy after they had gone to school somewhere else. Since 1987 the last Thursday in April is set aside for a memorial service at the tower to honor the memory of our Quincy natives who paid the ultimate sacrifice.

Bobby Phillips name was omitted from this memorial. I have been in contact with the Quincy Veterans Agency and pursuing an effort to have Bobby's name added to this memorial.

LETTERS TO MOM AND DAD

One thing that GIs value and look forward to most is a letter from home. Even though we are in a faraway place a short letter from family or friends makes us feel like we are still part of the real world. And conversely, a letter to our family or friends lets them know that we are alright. I had my mom, Jennie, for 68 years when she passed away in 2017. Like most moms, she was loving and caring and was the greatest cook I could imagine. Every meal was like a Sunday dinner and every Sunday dinner was like a holiday feast. I can still taste her homemade pasta and smell her unbelievable tomato sauce. On top of that she saved all of my baseball cards! After she passed, when I was cleaning out her closet, I found a shoe box in the far corner of a shelf. I just assumed it was an old pair of slippers or sneakers that she had forgotten about, and I was surprised when I opened it. In the box were all of the letters I had written home when I was in Vietnam. She had kept them after all of these years. I showed them to my son Patrick who ended up scanning them online and actually transcribing my somewhat legible cursive writing into a typed document. One thing that I noticed that I had forgotten about, was on each letter in the top corner I wrote in a number that reflected how many days I had left in country. Following are those letters. The words you see are verbatim, but for the sake of brevity where you see …………. it is basically something redundant or innocuous.

***

May 6, 1969   **363**

Hi,

Well, this is my second day in this country. It is really a strange place. I arrived at Cam Rahn Bay at 12:10am on Monday morning. When I got here it was 84 degrees, by mid- afternoon it was up to a 100. Today I moved down to Phu Ly where I was assigned to the 82nd Airborne Division. It's about 25 miles north of Saigon……………… So far it's been just like any other army base in the states, except that there is all sorts of barbed wire and sand bag bunkers around……….

Love, John

May 17, 1969   **352**

Hi,

Well I have been here 2 weeks. Everything is fine……….. I was sent to my Company today, we drove in a truck for about an hour and got to see a lot of the country. You couldn't believe the way these people live. Most of the houses are made out of cardboard and grass. We went through the outer part of Saigon and all you could see on the streets are bikes. I met a kid from Quincy. He lived in Montclair, but he is about 5 years older than me. We stayed up and drank beer one night until about 12 and I told him all about the changes in Quincy because he has been over here for 11 months……….Well that's all for now, everything is fine.

Love, John

May 23, 1969   **346**

Hi,

How is everyone? I was put in the 4th platoon in my company and they made me an RTO (Radio Telephone Operator). I carry a field radio on my back and stay with the platoon sergeant all the time………Nobody gives you any trouble, everyone is treated the same no matter what their rank. You don't even salute officers out here. Well that's all for now, say hi to everyone for me.

Love, John

May 29, 1969   **340**

Hi,

I got your letter the other day. I guess it takes 5 days for a letter to travel from Boston to here. Two guys from Quincy just came in. I know both of them. One was with me at Ft. Benning, Joe Harding and the other I went to North with, Brian Smith. I've also met 3 guys from my AIT unit. The monsoon season has just started here. It rains for about 2 or 3 hours and then it is good again. When it rains, the rice paddies get real muddy and it is brutal walking through them…………

When you send the package, put a tube of Clearasil in it. Well, say hi to everyone for me.

Love, John

June 2, 1969   337

Well I just got in from a 4 day operation. We came back to the base camp today and we'll be going back out tomorrow for 6 days. I have exactly 11 months to go now. That first month went pretty fast. When we're back at the base camp, we get 2 hot meals and one of C rations, but when we are out in the field we have 3 meals of C rations. But they're not regular C rations; they are dehydrated and all you have to do is add hot water and they taste pretty good. I got Diane's and Maryanne's letters. Well that's all for now.

Love, John

June 10, 1969   329

Hi,

How's everyone? I'm fine. We just got in from a 6 day operation. It wasn't to bad. I look great without shaving for 6 days. Dad is right about getting everything you need. Once a week, each platoon gets a box filled with cigarettes, candy bars, shaving gear and everything else we need, free...................I got a letter from Tommy Lacey, he is over here driving a truck. Why don't you start sending me the Patriot Ledger so I can see what's happening in the world.............That's all for now, say hi to everyone for me.

Love, John

June 13, 1969   326

Hi,

I got your letters................Where I am now we have a small river going by us so I go swimming every day. It's not the best place in the world to swim but it feels great over here. The paper money I sent is a Vietnamese dollar bill. They call it piaster. 118 piaster equals one U.S. dollar............Well that's all for now, say hi to everyone for me.

Love, John

June 14, 1969   325

Hi,

I got your package yesterday. Everything was intact. The guys loved your brownies. The orange juice tasted great in the morning. You didn't have to send soap or handkerchiefs. We get plenty of soap and there is no sense in keeping handkerchiefs because you can't get them laundered. The way it works here is the only clothes you have are the ones on your back. They bring clean fatigues out every 3 days and you just take what they have. You never get the right size or your own uniform. I'll use the handkerchiefs to clean my rifle, they're good for that. I want you to call Bill Cotter's house (in the book on Boltoph St) and get his address. He should be over here now.

Love, John

June 23, 1969   **316**

Hi,

Well I just got into the firebase from the field. We were out there for 7 days this time and we'll be back here in the firebase for 7 days now. This is the 3rd firebase I've been to. But they said we'll be working out of here for the next 6 months. One week in the field and one week in the firebase. But they could change it anytime. Our platoon is mostly new guys. Out of 23 men in our platoon, there is only 8 guys with more time than me and I've only been here for a month and a half. Well that's all for now. P.S. Tell Diane Happy Birthday and here's a Vietnam nickel.

Love, John

June 27, 1969   **312**

Hi,

Everything's okay, tell the guys down at the shop I said hi................We do most of our patrols at night. Each platoon sends out a 12 man ambush patrol every night. There is an ambush leader, a machine gunner, a grenade launcher, and 9 riflemen. I'm one of the riflemen, but I also carry the radio. We all carry about 20 magazines, a couple of grenades, trip flares and claymore mines. Plus everyone carries 100 rounds of machine gun ammo. We leave the perimeter just after dark and go about one mile out most of the time. This area is mostly rice paddies, so we set up behind a dike that separates the fields. But now we are in the middle of the monsoons, so it's to wet to set up behind them so we set up on top.........When we're back here at the firebase, they sometimes send men from each platoon on an overnight pass. I went in a couple of nights ago to Saigon. Some parts of it are beautiful with very modern buildings, and it looks like any big city in the states, but then you go to the lower part of the city and the sidewalks are crowded with people selling everything. One guy tried to sell me a 10 foot snake. You really can't do too much because there is a 10 o'clock curfew and everyone has to be off the streets. Well that's all for now.

Love, John

July 4, 1969   302
Hi,
Well we just got in from a 3 day operation near the Mekong Delta. From the second the helicopters brought us in to the second they took us out, we were soaking wet. It was all marshland and rice paddies. Well that's all for now. Say hi to everyone for me.

Love, John

July 9, 1969   297
Hi
How was your July 4th? We were in a firebase and we were shooting flares most of the night. I just got your package and I've gotten the Ledger also. I guess you're wondering about what I do with my money. Well, all I get paid is $50 a month. They put another $125 a month in the Soldier's Bank where it gets 10% interest and I carry forward about $20 they keep at the finance office. We just got a raise July 1. So I make another $17 a month starting this month. Well there's not much to write about so say hi to everyone for me.

Love, John

July 17, 1969   288
Hi,
How is everything? Everything is the same here. I could have gone to Hong Kong from Aug 8-15, but I didn't want to. It's called R and R (rest and relaxation) and everyone gets one the year they are over here.................I heard the Red Sox – Baltimore game on the radio the other day. It's on tape but you don't know the outcome until the games

over. The Red Sox lost, but Tony C hit 2 HR. **(As an aside, my son Patrick found the box score for the game I mentioned. It was July 13 and Baltimore won 6 – 3).** Well that's all for now. Hope everyone is in good health.

Love, John

July 22, 1969   **282**

Just writing to let you know I'm all right.........I read in the paper that Mathewson has a softball team in the Merchant's League. Is Dad playing for them? I noticed they were in last place. We had some guys from CBS here the other day. They were taking photos of the firebase we are at and interviewing some of the guys about the moon flight. They said it was going to be on TV as a special. I didn't get into it but some of the guys in my platoon did. Well that's all for now.

Love, John

August 9, 1969   **265**

I hope everyone is feeling good. We're down near the Mekong Delta again. We're going to be here for about a month. They took one company and assigned us to 3 companies of the Vietnamese Army. We have one platoon working with each company. They're pretty good soldiers, the only trouble is the language but you can usually get your point across. Well this summer has gone by pretty fast. In a couple of weeks the kids will be going back to school. I got a letter from Charlie (Mosher), he's with the 9th Div. and he says he might be leaving here next month and going to Hawaii to finish his tour. Well say hi to everyone for me.

Love, John

August 22, 1969   **254**

I know this is the first letter in about two weeks. We've been in the field for 22 straight days and will be here for four more days. Our whole battalion is in a place called the Pineapple Groves.........I bought a camera and took some pictures. I sent them home yesterday. When you get them developed, send them back to me so I can look at them........ Well say hi to everyone for me.

Love, John

September 8, 1969 **237**

Hi,

Well the summer is over now..........There's been rumors going around that the 82nd is going to be pulled out in Nov. or Dec. These rumors seem pretty true because they have been turning over all our firebases to the South Vietnamese soldiers and by the end of the month, they will have completely taken over our Area of Operation and they're going to put us somewhere else. So if things go right, I'll be home by Dec. Well it's still raining here, hasn't stopped since I got in country four months ago. Well that's all for now. Say hi to everyone for me.

Love, John

September 13, 1969 **232**

Well everything is still the same. If you can send me some Clearasil and some stamps, that's about all I need…………..

Love, John

September 16, 1969 **228**

Hi,

I got your package last night and as usual the brownies were great. I'm going on R+R to Sydney from Oct5 - Oct12. So that should be a good time. I'll have plenty of money so that's no problem……….

Love, John

September 23, 1969 **222**

Hi,

Well I hope you didn't get your hopes too high for me coming home. The 82nd is going home, but only the ones with over 6 months in country. I have just under 5. Out of 5,000 men over here in the 82nd about 1,500 are going home. They are assigning the rest of us to units over here….. I doubt if I'll be going to Australia on Oct 5th now. How does Ricky like Atlantic? And how does Maryann like North? Well that's all for now. Say hi to everyone for me.

Love, John

September 29, 1969 **216**

Hi,

…………….I found out today that I'll be going on R+R for sure Oct. 5th. So next Sunday I will be in Sydney. One of my buddies just came back and said it was great. I have about $400 in the company safe and I'll have about another $100 after I get paid, so when I get back from R+R I'll probably send some money home if I have any left. Hope everyone is feeling good.

Love, John

October 13, 1969 **201**

How is everyone? I got back from Sydney last night. It was the best time I ever had. It was just like being back in the States. Sydney is a fantastic place, the people are all friendly and the girls are all beautiful and wear the shortest mini-skirts in the world. I lived like a king. The hotel I stayed at was brand new, had radio, TV and a refrigerator in the room, breakfast in bed a heated swimming pool room service 24 hours a day. I met a guy named Steve Songa there. He lives on Bromfield St.

Well the 82nd is just about ready to go home. All of us that are staying here have our orders to our next unit. I'll be going to the 11th Armored Cav. It's a pretty good unit. I don't know what I'll be doing there, but it definitely will be better than what I had with the 82nd…………I also got promoted to Sp. 4. It's the same as a corporal. Now I make $292 a month. Well I hope everyone is feeling fine. Say hi to everyone for me.

Love, John

PS.

I won't be sending any money home seeing how I spent about $400.

November 3, 1969 **180**

Hi,

I 'm just writing a short note here. I need some stamps so I can send the film back to you………..Say Hi to everyone for me.

Love, John

November 12, 1969   **171**

Hi,

How's everything going? I got your package the other day and as usual
it didn't last very long. Well I've been in the 11th Cav for 3 weeks now
and so far it has the 82nd beat by a mile. We ride on APCs and we can
carry everything we need. We always have plenty of water, we carry cots
to sleep on and everything else we need we just throw into the track.
Right now, we are near a place called Bo Dup. It's about 3 miles from
the Cambodian border, and about 100 miles northwest of Saigon. This
area is completely different from the area I was in before. There are no
rice paddies, just giant rubber plantations. Just rows and rows of rubber
trees 60-70 feet high. The monsoon season is over now. It probably won't
rain for the rest of my time over here. It goes from one extreme to the
other. Well I guess it's starting to get kind of cool there now, over here
the hot season is just beginning. Well I hope everyone is ok and say hi
to them for me.

Love. John

November 21, 1969   **163**

Hi,

I just received your letter and glad to see everything is OK. I'll tell you
one thing, this unit has the 82nd beat by a mile. No more slogging through
the mud or sleeping in the rain. We ride everywhere in APCs. An
armored troop consists of about 25 APCs and 9 Sheridan tanks. Each
APC has a .50 cal and two .60 mm machine guns and the Sheridan tanks
have a .50 cal machinegun and fire a .152mm cannon. So as far as
firepower goes, you can't get much better than an armor unit.

Right now we are located about 2 miles from the Cambodian border,
100 miles NW of Saigon. We work with Special Forces and the S.
Vietnamese Army. They put a team of Green Berets with a company of
the SV Army and they work along side us. We don't spend any time in
firebases. We're always in the field. But it doesn't matter because we're
like a traveling firebase……..Well that's about it for now. Hope all's
well and say hi to everyone for me.

Love, John

November 28, 1969   **156**
Hi,
Hope you all had a happy Thanksgiving. We had a pretty good one here,
they brought out more food than we could possibly eat. All kinds of pies,
fruits and turkey we could eat. I also got your package yesterday, that
was good timing. The inside of my track looks like a pantry. There are
five of us and we all have received two packages in the last 45 days or
so that's 10 packages!...............Well that's about all for now. Just hope
everyone is feeling well and have a good holiday.
                                                        Love, John

December 14, 1969   **140**
Hi,
Well it's only 11 days from Christmas. It doesn't seem right with the
temp in the 90's and no snow. I got a package from the City of Quincy
Vietnam Assn. And I also got your package. For the last couple of weeks,
everyone is getting packages. Our track looks like a store with all the
canned goods stacked up. I sent a roll of film home the other day, you
should be getting it soon. The Ledger is coming regularly now. Well
there's not much to say. Hope everyone is okay and say hi to everyone
for me.
                                                        Love, John

December 25, 1969   **129**
Well Merry Christmas. It seems funny to say that. I'll be going on R+R
again to Sydney from Jan 28-Feb 4. I want you to send me a box with
just clothes in it ....Put in the brown shoes I sent home "not the
loafers" but the brown tie shoes. Also the two yellow shirts I sent home,
a button down collar and a polo. Put in two pair of pants, the black and
white checkered, and a pair of brown pants that I bought before I left.
Also put in a couple of my ties, a blue one and a tan one...... Well there's
not much more to say. Everything is still the same. Say hi to everyone
for me.
                                                        Love, John

January 9, 1970   **114**
Hi,
Just writing to let you know everything is ok. I got your letters and
packages. I'm going on R+R again because when I came into this unit, I
told them I hadn't been on R+R before and if I get a chance I'll go on
another. Well we've been out in the field ever since I came to this unit.
About 70 days…….I'm going to buy another camera. A Yashica 35mm.
It's a real good camera, a lot of guys buy them. Back in the states it would
cost $115 but over here it only costs $49, so I can't pass up a bargain like
that, well that's all for now, Hope everyone is feeling good.

Love, John

P.S As you can see by my return address, I got promoted again (SGT).

February 9, 1970   **83**
Well I guess it's been a long time since you got a letter from me. I've
been back from R+R for a few days now. I had another great time, I hated
to come back. But I only have about 2 ½ months left so it's not too bad.
I'm sending some pictures there the first I took with my new
camera……..I hope everyone is feeling okay.

Love, John

February 14, 1970   **78**
Just writing a few lines to let you know everything is alright………..I
just bought a kit to go along with my camera. It has a telephoto lens, a
wide angle lens filter and a few other things. Altogether, my camera and
kit costs $85, but in the states it would cost $220. I got a letter from Bill
Cotter the other day. He is doing okay. He decided to stay in the Army.
He's a captain, so he has it pretty good. How has North been doing in
basketball? Well that's about all I can think of for now. Say hi to
everyone for me.

Love, John

February 25, 1970   **67**
I'm glad you finally got my letter………………..Well I have just a little
over 2 months left. I should be home the first week in May. That's all for
now. Hope everyone's alright.

Love, John

March 14, 1970   **49**
How's everything going? I hope everyone is feeling good.............You said something about a movie camera in your last letter. I can definitely get one at a discount, if there is any special type or brand that you want to get just let me know and I'll get it. To give you an idea where I am located. It's Tay Ninh Province about 20 miles west of Tay Ninh city, the area is all bamboo and jungle. Well that's it for now. Say hi to everyone for me.

Love, John

***

So that's it; not a literary treasure, and I apologize to my English teachers at NQHS. I should have paid better attention to grammar, spelling and style. However, it is a sentimental gift and I am sure every GI would want to be able to look back and see what they sent home to their parents or wives. If you followed the thread closely, you would think that I was at a Boy Scout summer camp. I am sure if you saw letters from other soldiers they would mirror mine. The last thing we wanted was our loved ones to worry about us, the network news did too much of that. You should also notice how the frequency of letters changes. For the first six months I averaged about a letter a week. The last six months it was about a letter every two or three weeks. Besides getting physically fatigued, you also get mentally fatigued. The longer you are in country the more you get used to your new way of life so you are less motivated to write home.

My last letter indicated I had 49 days left in country. That was based on my scheduled rotation date of May 3, 1970. I actually left Vietnam on April 10, 1970, so my last letter would have been about 30 days before I left. That seems like a long time to go without writing. Maybe there is one more letter hidden somewhere in the house.

So thank you, Mom, for keeping the letters for all these years. Just another reason to love you. Well that's all for now. Hope everyone is okay and say hi to everyone up there for me.

Love, John

COMING HOME

Invariably the first thing I thought about when landing in South Vietnam was about the day that I would be leaving to come home. The tour of duty was one year and was arguably the longest year of my life. I didn't have a day planner to mark off my remaining days in country, but there were a couple of methods that I used to track my time left.

There are two types of Malaria that are common to South Vietnam, Falciparum and Vivax. Falciparum was deadly and Vivax merely made you sick, but there were preventative treatments. There was a little white pill for Falciparum that was 100% effective that we took daily and a larger pink pill for Vivax that was 50% effective that we took weekly. We were issued a year's supply when we entered in country and I put them all in a single pill bottle. I could then monitor my time left by simply shaking the bottle. Another way to measure time left was the traditional "short timer's calendar" commonly used by GIs since World War II. This tool was a one-page drawing of a voluptuous woman with 365 blocks covering her body that we would pencil in every day. It was an entertaining way to measure our progress and remind fellow GIs of the pecking order.

It was common practice in the 11th Armored Cav to be offered the opportunity to rotate out of the field and back to the safer rear area command base after being in country for ten months. I had reached my ten months, but decided to stay in the field. I guess it was a combination of being close with the guys that I had gone through so much with and not wanting to start over at the command base. However, with about five days left in my tour we were hit pretty hard with mortar fire and that convinced me that it was probably time to leave the field. The next morning I was on a chopper finally out of harm's way. It was an eerie feeling as the chopper lifted off the ground, and I saw the jungle beneath me disappear. Could I actually be back home by the end of the week? The rear command base was in Bien Hoa Airbase and was very safe. With only a few days left in country I wasn't assigned any duties so I spent that time drinking beer at the Enlisted Men's Club

My final day in country had arrived, but unlike World War II and Korea where GIs were transported on troop ships that took weeks to get home, in Vietnam we went home via commercial airlines complete with female flight attendants. There was still apprehension as I boarded the plane and waited for takeoff. "I have made it this far. Please don't let something crazy happen now." The plane made its way down the runway and I felt it lift off. The pilot came on the radio and announced, "Ladies and gentlemen, we have left South Vietnam." With that a loud cheer rose through the plane and I felt the tension leave my body. I really was on my way home.

There was a six-hour flight, and then refueling in Tokyo where I got off the plane and spent about three hours in a hangar. I got a hot meal and watched some TV for the first time in a year. I noticed that there were three tables set up at the far end of the hangar with about 20 GIs in line at each table. The three tables had displays of The Encyclopedia Britannica, The World Book Encyclopedia, and Great Books for sale. The soldiers were huddled with sales reps signing up for monthly payments to receive these reference books. At first I was impressed with the thirst for knowledge that my fellow soldiers were showing. But then I realized that these sales reps were some of the most beautiful women I had ever seen. It seems a soldier's thirst for knowledge is superseded by his desire to spend time with a pretty girl.

Nine hours later the coast of California appeared and I landed at Fort Ord just south of San Francisco. Another loud cheer went up when we touched down and the pilot announced that we had landed in the United States of America. Not only was my tour of duty in Vietnam over, but my time in the service had ended as well. Like most things in the Army bureaucracy, processing out took time. We went through final physicals, closing financial accounts, listening to re-enlistment overtures, and just plain sitting around. About 14 hours after landing I can finally leave the building. One benefit that I had, coming from Massachusetts, was that the Army paid our way back to our hometown from the base of discharge. They don't buy plane tickets, but give us 29 cents a mile, which in my case amounted to almost $900. With a military discount my plane ticket to Boston was only $150 leaving me with a nice profit.

On my next to last day in Vietnam I was reunited with my friend, Joe Casey from Woburn, MA whom I had met at the Combat Leadership School at Fort Benning, GA. In about two months I would be attending Joe's wedding, but here we were leaving the Army together. We could take a redeye flight to Boston in about 8 hours, but we decided to stay the night in San Francisco to see the sights and go home the next day. So we took the shuttle to the airport, checked into a hotel, went to our room, decided to take a quick nap, and woke up at midnight. So much for seeing the sights.

The next day I arrived in Boston around 5:00 pm, said goodbye to Joe, and took a taxi to Quincy. On the ride from Logan I started to recognize familiar sights and it finally hit me that I was really home. I arrived at my house just as the family was finishing dinner. There were a lot of hugs and kisses and yes, some tears. It was hard to believe that just a few days before mortar rounds were raining down on me and tonight I would be sleeping in my old bed.

I definitely had an adjustment period. I stayed inside my house for a few weeks just catching up on a year's sleep and still not fully grasping that I was home. I was content to be around my family and enjoy my mother's cooking. Eventually I ventured out and would walk down to Wollaston Beach. One day after about three weeks I was sitting on the sea wall, and a car stopped carrying three girls whom I had gone to high school with. Ellen, Maureen, and Sandy were just riding around and invited me to go along. I sat in the back seat with one of the girls not saying anything and listening to them jabber away. Even though we went to school together for some reason they suddenly seemed so very young. Finally one of the girls said, "Hey John, where have you been? We haven't seen you around." I told them I had just gotten back from a year in Vietnam. They were all quiet for a while and then the girl in the back seat gave me a sisterly hug and said, "I bet you're glad to be home." I said I was, and I held back the tears for all of those who wouldn't be able to say that.

Last day in country, boarding the Freedom Bird

ANOTHER VETERAN

If you didn't know him your first reaction would be, there is some old guy with thinning white hair hidden under a World War II ball cap stooped over as he shuffles behind his walker. You might wonder what kind of life he had led and maybe feel some sadness that time had passed him by. But those of you who have met him could attest that at 97 he still has his fastball! He is friendly and easy going, can express an opinion on any subject, and gets along with everyone. He has a great sense of humor and a complete recall of historic events. He loves coming to the Duxbury American Legion Post 223 on Veterans Day to reminisce with some of the other WWII veterans, like Leo Scarry, Jack Kelly, and before he passed away, Hank Reynolds. He is Romeo Magnarelli, and he is my dad.

You met my mother in a previous story and I mentioned I had her for 68 years. Here I am 72 years old and I still have a dad. I can remember him taking me to my first Red Sox game and getting Jackie Jensen's autograph. I can remember him going to all my football and basketball games in high school. I even worked with him for a year at Mathewson Machine works. Romeo worked for 42 years at Mathewson and retired when he was 63. He then started a second career working at local banks as a sanitary engineer. He ended up getting laid off from that job when he was 89! He had a work ethic second to none. But most of all I remember his loving relationship with his Jennie. Their meeting was right out of a Hollywood script. Romeo was in the Army training in Arkansas with his boyhood friend Ettore Lungari who he grew up with in South Quincy. Ettore noticed that Romeo was not getting much mail from home, so he suggested that Romeo write to this girl that he knew who lived in Quincy Point. Romeo wrote to Jennie Mariano often and when he got to meet her for the first time he knew she was the one for him. They were married for 71 years. One of my lasting memories of the two of them was from about five years ago. They would have both been 92. It was a warm summer morning and when I showed up at their house I knew that they were probably on the back deck having coffee. As I came around to the front of the deck I saw them and they were holding hands. They saw me and quickly let go of each other's hands as if they were teenagers caught by a parent. I tear up every time I think of that.

Like most veterans Romeo doesn't talk much about his time in the service even with me, someone who has had a similar military experience. However, he is an expert on this topic, with a collection of over 100 books on World War II. Every once in a while he points out something in one of his books and indicates that he was near that area or remembers something about that time. He only began regaling me with his accounts of the Army after he joined the Duxbury American Legion about eight years ago. As the Post 223 Adjutant, I talked to him about all of the activities that were going on at the Legion. I think that loosened him up.

One of his more interesting stories came about after the Duxbury 4th of July Parade in 2019. The parade is one of the highlights of the summer as it winds two-and-a-half miles down a tree-lined Washington Street and finishes in front of the high school beneath a 40-foot American flag flowing from the top of a fire department ladder truck. The dozens of large old colonial homes lining the parade route with white picket fences, expansive lawns, patriotic banners, and family cookouts is Americana at its best. Marching bands from as far away as Canada, dozens of themed neighborhood floats, and plenty of scout groups add to the festive atmosphere of the day. As is the tradition, the Duxbury American Legion Post 223 leads the procession. Our Legionnaires love the comradery and either march the route or ride in one of the many unique convertibles. Riding in a Robin's egg blue Volkswagen Beetle convertible driven by his daughter-in-law Pam, Romeo had a great time. The Legion was celebrating its 100th anniversary and had been chosen as the Grand Marshall which made the parade even more special. The parade route was packed with people both young and old, cheering the marchers and enjoying the activities. Romeo engaged the crowd the entire length, waving his flag, giving candy to the children, and flirting with the ladies. He had a smile that wouldn't quit.

After we returned home and had a few glasses of wine, he recounted what a great parade it was. He couldn't believe how many people were cheering and waving flags along the route. He told me that this was only the second parade he had ever been in. I had never thought about that. He had lived in Quincy all his life with many family and friends and attended many community events. I just assumed he would have been in a parade at some time.

As it turns out the only other parade he had participated in was on August 29th, 1944. On that day the Army's 28th Infantry Division marched down the Champs-Elysees, 24 men abreast with the Arc de Triomphe in the background as they liberated Paris. The men of the 28th had no idea of the magnitude of that historic moment. To them it was just easy duty given what they had gone through in the war.

The moment was captured in the most iconic photograph of World War II. You have probably seen it. If you look at the 3rd row from the bottom, on the left you will see a 20-year-old Romeo Magnarelli. Though the Duxbury 4th of July Parade is pretty special, it would have to go some to top Romeo's first parade.

The 28th Division had just come in from the battlefield and were going back out in two days. Little did they know that their journey would take them across France and into Belgium where they would partake in the bloodiest encounter of World War II, the Battle of the Bulge. Romeo would end up with the Combat Infantryman Badge, a Bronze Star, and two Purple Hearts. He would finish out the war marching all the way to Germany encountering many battles along the way. But for those two days, Paris was theirs and the French treated them like the heroes they were, especially the ladies.

But that is a story for another day!

Pam and Dad at Duxbury 4th of July Parade, 2019

EPILOGUE

The Vietnam War officially lasted almost 11 years, from August 1964 to May 1975. During that time over 9,000,000 American military personnel rotated through active-duty service somewhere around the world. Approximately 2,700,000 actually spent time in Vietnam, and 58,220 never made it home.

*25,493 gave their lives before they were legally eligible to order a drink at a bar in most states. 14,095 were 20 years old; 8,283 were 19 years old; 3,103 were 18 years old, and 12 were 17 years old.

*The Army sustained the most casualties with 38,224 killed; the Marines 14,844; the Air Force 2,586; the Navy 2,559; and the Coast Guard 7.

*49,830 of the fallen were white; 7,243 were African American; 368 were Asian or Pacific Islander; 349 were Hispanic; 226 were Native American; and 204 were multi-racial.

*The peak number of troops in country occurred in April of 1969 with 543,482.

*Massachusetts lost 1,331.

*The deadliest years were 1967 with 11,363 killed; 1968 with 16,899 killed; and 1969 with 11,780. That averages out to 256 deaths per week for 156 weeks.

*31 sets of brothers lost their lives as well as 3 fathers and sons.

*17,539 who lost their lives were married.

*382 committed suicide.

*The deadliest Military Occupation Specialty was, you guessed it, 11Bravo with 18,464 killed.

Statistics alone can't paint the impact the Vietnam War had on the American people. Just about everyone had a friend, neighbor, classmate, or relative who paid the ultimate sacrifice. But you have to put a face or name to the 58,220 to truly feel their loss. Though the war was a half century ago, the legacy of Vietnam is with us every day. Hopefully some of these stories have touched you in a positive way that will keep the memories alive for those we lost.

"All gave some and some gave all."
May they all rest in peace.

ABOUT THE AUTHOR

John Magnarelli grew up in North Quincy, Massachusetts and was drafted into the Army on August 12, 1968. After his tour of duty in the Army he went on to receive a Bachelor's and Master's Degree in Business Administration from Suffolk University in Boston. He had a 36-year career with the U.S. Department of Agriculture's Food and Nutrition Service, and for the last 27 years was the Regional Director overseeing the National School Lunch Program and nine other feeding programs for the six New England states and the state of New York. In addition to his time with the U.S. Department of Agriculture, he was a high school football referee for 46 years, elected to two terms on the Duxbury, MA school board, and for the last eight years has been the Adjutant General of the Duxbury American Legion Post 223. John and his wife Pam currently live in Plymouth, MA.

Sergeant John Magnarelli
Republic of Vietnam
May 4, 1969 – April 10, 1970

Decorations
Bronze Star for Valor
Combat Infantryman's Badge
Vietnam Cross of Gallantry
Vietnam Service Medal
Vietnam Campaign Medal
Army Commendation Medal
National Defense Service Medal